ENCOUNTERING THE OTHER

Borgo Press Books by FRANCIS JARMAN

Culture and Identity (editor)
Encountering the Other (editor)
The Gate of Lemnos: A Science Fiction Novel
Girls Will Be Girls: A Play
Intercultural Communication in Action (editor)
Invictus: A Play
Lip Service: A Play
A Star Fell: A Play
White Skin, Dark Skin, Power, Dream: Collected Essays on Literature & Culture

ENCOUNTERING THE OTHER

FRANCIS JARMAN,

EDITOR

THE BORGO PRESS
MMXI

**Borgo Perspectives on
Intercultural Communication**

Number One

ENCOUNTERING THE OTHER

Editing Copyright © 2011 by Francis Jarman
Individual essays Copyright © 2011 by the authors.

FIRST EDITION

Published by Wildside Press LLC

www.wildsidebooks.com

DEDICATION

For K.

CONTENTS

INTRODUCTION: THE OTHER, by Francis Jarman 9

ENCOUNTERING THE OTHER AS DISCOVERING
    ONESELF, by Peter Graf 17

(NOT) SO PLEASED TO MEET YOU: THE EARLY
    YEARS IN GERMANY, by Ellin Burnham 33

IMAGES OF AMERICA: A PERSONAL ACCOUNT, by
    Rainer Barczaitis 43

AMERICA: "A CITY UPON A HILL"? A
    PERSONAL VIEW, by Jürgen Einhoff 63

DAYS IN THE LIFE OF AN EXPAT, by Hans Schmidt . . 87

MY BIG FAT GREEK WORK EXPERIENCE, by Silvia
    Grimmsmann 93

THE WANDERING FOREIGNER AND A CONFLICT
    OF CULTURES, by Mayuri Odedra-Straub 107

YOU, ME, AND "HUM," by Manju Ramanan 119

THE POOPING QUEEN: REFLECTIONS ON THE
    OWN AND THE OTHER, by Paul Harrison 133

IRAQ 2003: A TALE OF INTERCULTURAL MISUNDERSTANDINGS, by Francis Jarman 153

THE DEVELOPMENT OF POLITENESS AS "SOCIAL CURRENCY" IN BRITAIN, THE USA AND BULGARIA, by Emilia Slavova 169

POLITENESS PHENOMENA IN ENGLAND, GERMANY AND SPAIN: AN APPROACH TO THE HIDDEN RULES OF BEHAVIOR, by Guadalupe Ruiz Yepes 191

CONFLICT OVER LAUNDRY: THE CULTURE OF WASHING IN GERMANY AND SWEDEN, by Anne-Kristin Langner. 201

THE FRENCH PLAY OF SEDUCTION, by Isabelle Kross 213

"QUEER" OTHERNESS, by T. W. Geraghty 223

ABOUT THE AUTHORS 231

INTRODUCTION
THE OTHER

THE OTHER IS truly not like us—how else to explain our nervousness, even fear, in its presence?

Sometimes it's about **appearance**. The appearance of Africans, their features and their skin-color, was found disturbing by many early modern Europeans. The ancient Greeks, however, had no such problem. Sir Alfred Zimmern (1911) dismissed the idea in a magisterial footnote: "The Greeks thought negroes *very interesting-looking people* and were amused at their woolly hair, but they show no trace of 'color-prejudice'" (323, footnote 1, my emphasis). A substantial documentation of ancient attitudes to race can be found in Snowden (1970).

Equally disturbing (and distasteful) was the appearance of Europeans to many non-Westerners. The former tended to be seen to resemble ghosts or devils—the Cantonese term for "Caucasian", *gwailo*, literally means "ghost man"—and their comparative hairiness and sweatiness was often found alarming. To Japanese, the Westerners were *bata-kusai* ("stinking-of-butter"; Koreans, on the other hand, are "garlic stinkers"), and I well remember being followed down a street in provincial Thailand by small children, who pulled at the hair on my forearms, delightedly shouting "Monkey! Monkey!"

The classical world lacked that "fundamental race distinction which became a marked characteristic of American negro slavery of the eighteenth and nineteenth centuries" (Westermann

1955, 11). There was no mutually reinforcing semantic linkage of race, slavery and inferiority, since slaves in antiquity could be recruited from any social class and from any ethnic group. Nor was there any need to **dehumanize** them in order to exploit them, as the Christian world later found it necessary to do with Africans, who were, as Rousseau (1761) put it, "transformed into beasts, for the service of the rest" (vol. II, 207). This strategy of dehumanizing human beings in order more easily to instrumentalize them is not unique to the West, however—during the Second World War, the prisoners subjected to unspeakable "experiments" by Unit 731 of the Japanese Army in Manchuria were known as *maruta*, or "logs of wood" (Daws 1994, 259).

Tzvetan Todorov (1982) has described the three major axes along which we plot alterity as follows: there is the *value judgement*, or "axiological level", of superiority or inferiority; the "praxeological level" of *identification* (do I find myself in the Other, or do I impose on the Other my own values and identity?); and there is the "epistemic level" of *knowledge* (or ignorance) of the Other (185). The Europeans who first encountered the indigenous peoples of America effectively used two strategies for coping with their alterity and incorporating them into their own Christian world-view: either the native peoples were radically different, and **intrinsically inferior**, or else they were similar to Europeans, though at an earlier, **less developed** stage (which could even be romanticized, at a safe distance, in the Edenic trope of the "Noble Savage"). "What [was] denied [was] the existence of a human substance truly other, something capable of being not merely an imperfect state of oneself" (42). For the native Americans, it was something of a no-win situation.

The Other has not always been viewed so essentialistically. The Greeks seem to have been more disturbed by the inability of "barbarians" to speak Greek properly, if at all—other considerations of inferiority could proceed from that unforgivable **linguistic failing**. Even those who spoke dialect, or less than perfect Greek, came in for scorn. In his fierce anti-Macedonian speeches, Demosthenes lambasted King Philip of Macedon as a "barbarian"—"Is not Philip our enemy? And in possession of our property? And a barbarian? Is any description too bad for him?" (*Third Olynthiac*, 51), indeed,

> he is not only no Greek, nor related to the Greeks, but not even a barbarian from any place that can be named with honor, but a pestilent knave from Macedonia, whence it was never yet possible to buy a decent slave (*Third Philippic*, 241, 243).

And the supposedly corrupt form of Greek spoken by the citizens of Soli, in distant Cilicia, gave rise to a term, *soloikismos*, that has survived in English as "solecism".

Catastrophically and fatally wrong **religious belief** could and still can be sufficient to place other members of the human race beyond the pale, in the ranks of those to be exterminated without mercy. For centuries, this was the driving impulse of both Christianity and Islam, as when, around 1410, the Turkish poet Ahmedi defined the *ghazi*, the Muslim "sword of God", as "the instrument of the religion of Allah, a servant of God who purifies the earth from the filth of polytheism" (quoted in Luttrell 1965, 139; "polytheism", because of the Christian belief in the Trinity), or when, during the Albigensian Crusade, the warrior abbot Arnald-Amaury of Citeaux, frustrated, at the sack of Béziers (1209), by the confusing physical and cultural similarity of the Cathar heretics to the crusaders, supposedly gave his troops the instructions: "Kill them all! God will recognize His own!" (quoted in Sumption 1978, 93).

Unfortunately, it remains even in modern times the view of fundamentalists that non-believers (as *they* define them) will burn in Hell for all eternity, a view that can be supported by reference to the sacred books, *e.g.*,

> But the fearful, and *unbelieving*, and the abominable, and murderers, and whoremongers, and sorcerers,

and *idolators*, and all liars, shall have their part in the lake which burneth with fire and brimstone: which is the second death (*Holy Bible, Revelation,* 21: 8, Authorized King James Version, my emphases),

or, from a different religious perspective: "Lo! Allah hath cursed the disbelievers, and hath prepared for them a flaming fire, / Wherein they will abide for ever" (*Holy Koran,* Sura 33: *Al-'Ahzab (The Allies)*, 64 f., in the Pickthall translation); yet at least the miserable non-believing creatures have the means to salvation—conversion—within their own power.

It might be said that interaction between the **generations** occasionally has something of the nature of communication across cultural barriers, involving as it may do an encounter with almost incomprehensible values and attitudes; and there is a well-established school of thought that tends to see the (failure of) **gender** communication between men and women in a similar light (see the works of Deborah Tannen, or popular best-sellers like John Gray's *Men Are from Mars, Women Are from Venus*). In their book *Seeing the Big Picture* (2006), which offers a "cinematic approach to understanding cultures in America", Ellen Summerfield and Sandra Lee include **gay culture** and **deaf culture** alongside the hyphenated American cultures. But the focus of these essays will be on a more narrowly and traditionally defined "intercultural communication", and—with an occasional glimpse in a different direction, as in the final essay, for example—on the encounter with **a cultural or ethnic Other**.

THIS IS THE first book in a series with the broader title *Borgo Perspectives on Intercultural Communication.* The essays in this first volume fall into two rough categories—**personal accounts** of encounters with cultural Otherness; and **interactions**, in such areas as social politeness, everyday contact, seduction, and war.

The Other that is encountered here is more often close-by than distant and exotic. We do occasionally have moments of contact and mutual incomprehension with the spectacularly alien. In my own experience, there was, for instance, the two-way bemusement that occurred when, on my first day in Japan (and not in Tokyo, but in a provincial city), I ventured out shopping and needed to explain what it was that I was looking for (in some cases they seemed to want to know *why* I was looking for it)—it wasn't a purely linguistic problem, it was also about aesthetics and values. Or there was the amazed stand-off with Bhil tribal herdsmen, encountered on a hill-track in a remote part of northwest India, who had never seen a "white man" before, just as I had never experienced anything like them either. I managed to capture something of their bafflement in a couple of photographs; unfortunately, no-one was able to record mine.

Stories like these make for good travellers' tales, but this extreme strangeness is less fundamentally disturbing (if only because we can barely relate to it, and are immediately aware of our incapacity) than the half-familiar, the *faux ami* that tricks us into believing that we understand it and then lets us know in brutal fashion that its patterns and values are not the same as ours. That hurts much more.

Most of the contributors to this volume are colleagues, former colleagues, former students or friends of mine (these are overlapping categories) from the University of Hildesheim in Germany, but there are also contributions from further afield. The authors come from Britain, Bulgaria, France, Germany, India, Ireland, Kenya, Spain and the United States, although this is to oversimplify somewhat, as several of them are of rather complex mixed ethnicity.

Among the topics, there are essays on the perception and significance of "Otherness" (GRAF; RAMANAN; GERAGHTY); personal takes on the United States (by Germans: BARCZAITIS; EINHOFF), on Germany (by an American: BURNHAM), on Greece (GRIMMSMANN), on a number of different countries (HARRISON; ODEDRA-STRAUB), and even on an unnamed culture (SCHMIDT)— the reader being challenged to identify which country is meant;

and studies of specific features of everyday life in France (KROSS) and Sweden and Germany (LANGNER), of politeness in England, Germany and Spain (RUIZ YEPES) and in Britain, the United States and Bulgaria (SLAVOVA), and of the intercultural misunderstandings that characterized the Second Gulf War (JARMAN).

The listings of "References" at the end of some of the contributions are precisely that—listings of works directly referred to or quoted from—and are not intended to be full academic bibliographies. Where online sources are given, the date of most recent access is uniformly January 20th, 2011.

The views expressed in individual essays are not necessarily those of the editor, the publisher or any of the other contributors.

FORTHCOMING VOLUMES IN the series will be about *Intercultural Communication in Action*, with essays about the internet, media and journalism, education, and language, and about *Culture and Identity*.

The series has two "homes". The first is the Institute of Intercultural Communication at Hildesheim University, Germany, which is where I happen to teach and research. The second is Wildside's Borgo Press, where I should particularly like to thank my editor, Professor Michael Burgess, for his encouragement, support and unfailing patience.

—FRANCIS JARMAN
Hildesheim, Germany
January 2011

References

Daws, Gavan. *Prisoners of the Japanese: POWs of World War II in the Pacific*. New York: William Morrow, 1994.

Demosthenes. *Demosthenes I: Olynthiacs, Philippics, Minor Public Speeches, Speech against Leptines, I-XVII, XX*. Transl. J. H. Vince. Cambridge, MA: Harvard University Press, 1930.

Gray, John. *Men Are from Mars, Women Are from Venus: A Practical Guide for Improving Communication and Getting What You Want in Your Relationships* (1992). New York: HarperCollins, 1993.

Luttrell, Anthony. "The Crusade in the Fourteenth Century." In: *Europe in the Late Middle Ages*. Ed. John Hale / Roger Highfield / Beryl Smalley. London: Faber & Faber, 1965, 122-54.

Rousseau, Jean-Jacques. *Eloisa, or, A Series of Original Letters* [*La nouvelle Héloïse*, 1761]. English translation in three volumes. Volume two. London: John Harding *et al.*, 1810.

Snowden, Frank M., Jr. *Blacks in Antiquity: Ethiopians in the Greco-Roman Experience*. Cambridge, MA: Harvard University Press, 1970.

Summerfield, Ellen / Lee, Sandra. *Seeing the Big Picture: A Cinematic Aproach to Understanding Cultures in America*. Ann Arbor, MI: University of Michigan Press, 2006.

Sumption, Jonathan. *The Albigensian Crusade* (1978). Paperback edition. London: Faber & Faber, 1999.

Todorov, Tzvetan. *The Conquest of America: The Question of the Other* [*La Conquête de l'Amérique*, 1982]. Transl. Richard Howard. New York: Harper & Row, 1985.

Zimmern, Alfred. *The Greek Commonwealth: Politics and Economics in Fifth-century Athens* (1911). Fifth edition. Oxford: Oxford University Press, 1931.

ENCOUNTERING THE OTHER AS DISCOVERING ONESELF

BY PETER GRAF

"Man becomes I through You."
—*Martin Buber*

SINCE ERIK H. ERIKSON, adolescence has been regarded as the decisive stage in the human development of identity. It is during this period of life that the experience of the formation of identity is confronted by that of the diffusion of identity. The central, vital problem that motivates young adults during this stage of their lives revolves around the question: "Who am I within the community" (Erikson 1959, 215). And it is in order to find an answer to this that they leave the family and become involved with people who were previously strangers to them. Is it not odd that, in order to find out who they are, young adults all over the world and from all cultural backgrounds leave behind them everything that they are familiar with, everything that they could call their own, including the safe and familiar circle of their family, even when that has taken good care of their needs? Beyond this familiar world of their own, they will discover who they are by encountering the Other, and find out how their identity might develop in community with others. Setting out on this course of development implies for young adults parting from familiar settings and crossing common borders, a process which is often painful. Not only young men and women, but also people in migration, yes, even entire nations, are nowadays faced with the task of crossing the borders of the Own, of a way of life that derives from their country of origin or a trusted national order, in order to shape their identity in a different setting and represent convincingly where they've come from in an international context.

1.0 Formation of Personality by Relationship: the Anthropology of Martin Buber

IT IS IMPOSSIBLE to find your own identity, to develop an individual personality, except in relation to others, although it might often be assumed that the initial task for an individual person would be to establish a profile of onself before making any approach to others. But the anthropological concept of the philosopher Martin Buber (1973) makes the assumption that such a process of learning has to turned round if it is to succeed: *Man becomes I through You* (32). Martin Buber does not assign the relation of I and You to the field of ethics or see it as a normative form of the relation to others. According to Buber, man is only able to recognize his own self in and through relationships with others. Entering into relations with other people is part of an anthropological concept. Turn into who you are together with others; recognize yourself in the mirror of the other person! This is the mission of the "dialogical principle", as Buber summarizes his concept. He introduces it in the following way:

> The attitude of man is twofold in accordance with the two basic words he can speak. The basic words are not single words but word pairs. One basic word is the word pair I-You. The other basic word is the word pair I-It: but this basic word is not changed when He or She takes the place of It (7).

The German word for "twofold" (*zwiefältig*) is related to the word for "doubt" (*Zweifel*), and correspondingly raises the question of having to decide between two choices. According to Buber, no one is able to imagine his own self except in connection with some sort of relation to another person: either entering into relation with this person in the form of a "You" or relating to him in the form of an "It", an object. This pair of words is vital in determining the formation of personality, because: "Man cannot live without the 'it'. But he who lives with 'it' alone, is not a man" (38). The realization of one's own self consists in entering into personal relations with others in a world in which "it"-functionality is constantly increasing. Whereby men have no choice whether to enter into relations with others or not, because, as Buber puts it: "All actual life is encounter" (15). Human existence is born in relations and ends there: "In the beginning there is relation" (31). When Buber, the Bible translator, refers clearly and repeatedly to this "Being in relation" with the term "beginning" (*principium*), he means with this the principle of the origin and essence of human beings. However, what is the I-You-relation all about? It goes beyond any objective, any functional reason for the relation to others. It is both "inclusive" and "exclusive" at the same time, and experienced in togetherness, because: "The basic word I-You can only be pronounced with one's entire essence" (15). At the same time, no one can dispose purely as he wishes of his relation to the "You": "Relation is reciprocal. My 'You' affects me in the same way as I affect it" (19). At this point it becomes clear that the other person to whom one relates will necessarily always remain "Other" in the sense of being elusive. Relation originates from a "primordial distance"; mutual reasons are given for each other.

This anthropological concept goes far beyond the common recommendation to approach the Other with tolerance. Beyond ethical norms this implies a never-ending process of self-recognition in the mirror of the Other up to and including mutual silence (41). The dramatic character of Buber's position is not least due to the fact that, as a member of the Jewish minority, he developed this concept in times when German civilization was already on fire. What he is here concerned with is an existentially vital process of recognition necessary for everybody but which nobody disposes of alone and which is not possible without awareness of the *Dazwischen*, the "interhuman in-between": "Spirit is not in the I, but between I and Thou. It is not like the blood that circulates in you, but like the air in which you breathe" (41). This is why Buber insists on the cognitive necessity for all participants to enter into a dialogical relationship that will change them on the basis of their difference and thus enable them to recognize their personal identity. Individuation calls for personal relation within a dialogue. The relation reveals where and how the own self is distinguished from others.

> Any true relation in the world comes out of the process of individuation; [...] within a perfect relation my You covers my Self without representing it; the limits of my recognition will be opened into a having been recognized without limits (101).

2.0 Finding the Self within the Other: the Social-psychological Context

HOW DO PEOPLE unfold their own self? George H. Mead, Erik H. Erikson und Erving Goffman regard this as a process of learning that holds true for all individuals. I would like to summarize this in terms of the following three dimensions:

2.1 Identity as a Process of Life-long Learning

Man does not possess identity, he has to look for it and develop it—during the entire span of his life-time. Therefore he who derives his identity from the facts of his own achievements is following a pathogenic concept that prevents further development. Development is furthered by repeated crises that involve the need to transcend levels already achieved. In this way, the learning of identity becomes an integral part of one's life and a path towards the realization of one's self.

2.2 Identity as Interaction and Relation

No person is able to find his identity on his own: he will only achieve this in interaction with and in relation to others. The self-image is only convincing when discovered as a reflection in the mirror of the Other. Nobody fixes his identity before turning his attention to the Other. On the contrary, he only realizes what he might be through the reaction of others. This is the reason why young people of necessity have to leave their families and form new relationships, in order to know who they really are.

2.3 Identity as Symbolic Exchange

The question "Who am I?" finds its answers in linguistic-symbolic communication. This requires a differentiated common language and in addition the readiness to listen to one another attentively and to the point of mutual silence in mutual open-mindedness. Poetry and art find their determinant value in the exchange of significations and signs: For thousands of years and from generation to generation, human beings have interpreted their world and their place within the community by means of stories and texts, songs and music, art and expression.

3.0 Intercultural Learning as Leave-taking

LIVING TOGETHER WITH immigrant groups in societies with migration and living in a globally networked world calls for a readiness to go beyond the familiar patterns of cultural behavior. New, convincing identities can only be found in the beyond, after the farewells have been made. In the words of Erik H. Erikson: "The forming of identity really begins at that point where the usefulness of the identifications ends" (140).

3.1 Abandon Conceit and Pride in One's Own Peculiarities

It is time to part from reified concepts of identity such as people are "proud" of. Such things as are derived from the self prevent the act of entering into relation. This is why we have to part from national, cultural or religious concepts which take the own as the criterion by which other groups are measured. Outward qualities in general do not suffice; they are only an impetus for internal processes: This is why it is also not good to place identity on multicultural, transnational or inter-religious foundations via new terminological schemata.

3.2 Remove the Partition Walls between Groups

It is also necessary to part from cultural barriers that pretend to guarantee the order of the world. Just as transparent partitions determine in public life who is entitled to get into contact with whom, and how, cultural dividing walls hinder communication in both directions and prevent interpersonal encounters. At present, characteristics of behavior and of dress take over the separating function of partitions. They speak of difference, and indicate what kind of contacts will be accepted and which will be rejected.

3.3 No Further Exclusion of Serious Topics

Communication will only be of interpersonal significance if each partner is allowed to ask all the questions that are essentially important to him. Often, religious institutions will only permit certain topics in situations of interreligious dialogue. It is not only the Vatican that demands that interreligious dialogue be restricted to cultural and moral topics, and avoid questions of faith. In contrast, Buber called long ago for a "genuine religious dialogue" that does not end where serious matters begin and central questions are raised (Buber, 149).

3.4 No More Disguises

Admitting insights in order to build a world together, instead of leaving it to forces of destruction, does not entail an artificial construct afloat on idealism. It is the only significant reality that we have: a mutual interpretation of the world that originates from our inner selves. Human cognition is a living construct that is shaped in cooperation with others. It not only reflects the external world, but expresses an internal one too. Thus it is artists who worldwide, and more openly than others, reveal in their works the depth of the experience of human existence. Past and present, they present man in his nakedness and simplicity and thus reveal the structures of our inner cognition to others.

4.0 Identity as Individuality

THE SEARCH FOR identity implies asking onself such questions as each individual—as an indivisible unity (Latin: *in-dividuum*, Greek: *atomo*, person)—must answer for himself. These answers cannot be required from someone else, or from an institution. Nobody will know the other person well enough to have the right to pass judgement on his identity. The times are coming to an end in which others are able to define how people's lives should be assessed, beyond the general norms of law. Instead, people are to be encouraged to set out on their individual journey in order to find themselves, together with and in relation to others.

4.1 Internal Orientation

On the road to discovering his own identity man requires an inner map of orientation, the coordinates of which are synchronized with his environment. Such a map will enable the person to build a sensible continuum across his own biography and help him to build bridges of comprehension to his environment. Such maps of orientation are only convincing, if they do not contain blank areas, and do not exclude anybody or any part of the given world. Contrary to this principle, the present state of relations between people from different faiths is still overshadowed by prohibitions, including the fiercest possible sanctions in cases where the "wrong" marital partner is chosen. It is here that the serious and dramatic character of intercultural dialogue becomes particularly evident for young adults, who have to meet the challenges of their environment and set out to discover, together with others, their own self—a journey comparable to a joint lift-ride up a steep mountain.

4.2 The Personal Challenge

Identity appears to be both an individual search and a common journey. The challenge could hardly be a greater one. The horizon and periphery in which the way is to be found is without margin or limit. The environment in which this task is to be realized is alive and constantly changing. The partners on this road not only create a context, they are also teachers who accompany you on the journey.

IN THE END, the search for one's identity cannot go too deep. And this is why intercultural learning implies the following: there is no way to determine the surroundings of the periphery; the center is always where you yourself are. There is no higher task to be undertaken than to experience your own self around the deep personal core of your existence, which only you can approach. The seriousness of the task lies in the following: that it permits neither perception of the environment in terms of an emic/etic perspective nor the adoption of the distanced viewpoint of the "observer", as is so often proposed in systems theory. Awareness of the Self is not something that stands in contrast to the outside world; it is something which is created, always new, out of life's ever-changing experience of difference (see Graf 2002, 323 f.).

5.0 Identity as Being Different

AS EARLY AS the fourteenth century Master Eckhart was urging his pupils: "Set off in order to return" (see Graf / Unterreitmeier 1992). He who never goes to other places will never know who he can be and where he can go. The unfamiliar will teach him to realize who he is by showing him who he is not. He who is being asked about his identity is often only able to say who he is not and in which way he differs from others. There is nothing wrong with this, since according to Gregory Bateson (1972) any piece of information is significant only in so far as that it is a "difference that makes a difference" (582). And this presupposes two systems. In general, our cognition is adjusted for processing differences. Thus we are able to perceive the depth of a space by the difference between the images from the left and the right eye. The hand of a clock can only tell us that it is a particular time, if we happen to know where it is on the clock face. In the search for our identity, our personal expectation only becomes significant if we know the other's reply to it, and whether the answer matches our expectation or not—and here it is the latter that is of utmost importance. Cognition happens at the interface of expectation and fulfilment. According to Goffman (1963), identity originates "in relations" which stretch between on the one hand the "virtual social identity" and on the other the "actual social identity", which is fulfilled by oneself (10). Both poles are always different, reminding the individual to shape his self within the tension of difference. Groups that do not admit these differences in the *Dazwischen* (the interhuman in-between) prevent the formation of personal identity.

5.1 Human Cognition as Processing of Difference

The entire human neuronal network—from the nerves to the brain—is conditioned to process difference. Neurons can only signal difference, via On- and Off-centers that stand in relation to each other, in the form "no longer the same as previous" or "here not in the same way as in the neighboring position" (Hubel 1988, 50). Human cognition originates from a millionfold comparison of neuronal signals at each moment of our perception. When following a film, we see a movement that our brain produces by comparing a sequence of standing pictures. When distinguishing infinite shades of color we recognize these by processing in a comparative manner the impulses that stem from the optic cells for three basic colors and the brightness value. Finally, our brain is divided into two hemispheres in order to process differently similar signals of the senses and to produce by this way the endless variety of our cognition from the difference perceived in it.

Not only does this biologically-based general structure of human cognition facilitate the infinite range of human perception. According to Humberto R. Maturana and Francisco J. Varela (1984) it also forms the basis for all those constructive processes that characterize our perception. In addition, this school of cognitive psychology underlines the immense importance of groups and communication with others by pointing to the fact that we learn from others how to speak and that there are always differences between the answer and the question. The omnipresent differences between the speakers, their experience and knowledge lay the foundation for the unlimited possibilities of human opinion, expressed with others and in a common language.

5.2 Collective Co-ontogeny in Communication with Others

Men are born from relations, they are not able to survive without a social environment, and they are unable to learn their specific social and linguistic abilities without a group. According to Maturana and Varela, man becomes a person during his development of language and consciousness through a collective form of co-ontogeny (207ff.). In this process, human cognition appears as a result of social structural coupling via language, leading to an expansion of human consciousness. Varela (1990) considers linguistic communication "not as a tool of communication, but as a network by which we define ourselves as individuals" (113). If human identity derives from common language, it will be continuously accentuated by the questions put forward by others and differentiated in its significance every time in a unique and individual manner: "What biology shows us is that the uniqueness of being human lies exclusively in a social structural coupling that occurs through languaging" (Maturana / Varela, 246).

In their line of argumentation, both authors proceed even further: Human cognition, in the form of reflection on one's own perception, produces a concept of personal identity, which is formed internally, since cognition is initiated by outside stimuli but is the result of contructive inner processing. It is an effective form of action, which people opt for internally and according to their physical constitution. In this way, they continuously *produce themselves* in a constructive process. Thus, cognitive psychology points to a form of internal reflection based on social exchange which continuously approaches the core of the self but without grasping it. Intelligent persons are not able to determine their identity in a few sentences. And this is not what it is about. According to Varela, men were not given their intellect in order to answer some questions in a statically determinant manner, but "in order to enter into a world shared with others" (111). Accordingly, Maturana and Varela conceive human cognition as a continuous process of constructing significance, to be carried out together with others:

> We have delved into a social dynamics which points up a basic ontological feature of our human condition that is no longer a mere assumption, that is, *we have only the world that we bring forth with others, and only love helps us bring it forth* (248, italics in the original).

6.0 Theses for Discovering the Self within the Other

THE APPEAL TO "Know Thyself", advanced in ancient Greece to a principle of Western philosophy, leads to an amazing convergence in modern anthropology, social psychology and cognitive psychology. This high task, indeed, the highest challenge facing any person, has gained new relevance interculturally.

6.1 Finding Oneself as the Task of the Individual

When it comes to discovering one's own self, everyone is on their own. Human cognition is not restricted to the reception and reproduction of objects, but is an action that comes from within, from inside your body, from your own biography and in community with others. In this manner, every person gains a unique conception of his individual self, so as is not to be found repeated in any other person. And this is why no group or nation, no religious or cultural community, has the right to determine the identity of one of its members on his behalf. Anyone who determines the identity of others on their behalf in a reified manner prevents them from developing a true self.

6.2 Enculturation as Cognitive Map

No one is able to set out on his way without a cognitive map of orientation: whom does he want to go with, in which direction, and how far? This is the first challenge of enculturation faced by young adults. In general, this entails a map of orientation related to the first language, the family, culture and religion, a map which everybody needs and which therefore has to be acquired. This first map, however, may not show blank spaces that remain forever unknown or set up borders to the outside, as this would deprive the map of scope and validity, ruling out any exploration of new worlds as well as deeper reflection about one's own location in the midst of everything. It doesn't lead to a better understanding of one's own language if the learning of other languages is forbidden. Maps of cultural orientation actually fulfil their purpose better if they enable their user to follow new paths independently.

6.3 Communication without Partition Walls

According to the insights of modern psychology, all people worldwide can now enter into comprehensible communication with each other, in the same way and without any restriction. This implies mutual recognition on the same level, beyond any linguistic, cultural or religious borderlines. In cognitive-psychological terms, all men draw on the same sources. This inner relatedness offers a connection to all other people that is deep and open to everyone in the world. As different as the world's cultures may be in their ways of shaping life, they rest on mental foundations that unite all of us. The wider the cultural gap may be, the more intensive will be the task of coping with difference and the more surprising will be the new insights gained. There is only one way to achieve this: by entering into relation and by dedicating your full commitment. And: the wider the gap, the more enormous will be the area of new experience opened up by such recognition. He who responds to the questions posed by the Other will assume co-responsibility with him for the shaping of the world, because "The knowledge of this knowledge constitutes the social imperative for a human-centered ethics" (Maturana / Varela, 246).

6.4 Construction of a World of Meaning

Human cognition as the recognition of a meaningful world is a continuous process which is constantly re-made in cooperation with others. Consequently, the mutually produced world of meaning is always shaped in a constructive manner, or left to be eroded by destructive powers. Considering the fact that human life and insight are never stagnant and never pause, there is no other alternative. It is not mere inaction if one ignores impulses from the outside or refuses the exchange with certain groups, no, it is an active contribution to decay and destruction. If culture and religion are forms of life to be shaped by man, there is no static "final stage" that, once reached, has to be preserved. As a lived expression of common meaning it always needs to be reproduced anew, together and in communion with others.

And this is what reveals the dramatic character and existential relevance of the intercultural dialog as a crossing of borders. During encounters with strangers, hardenings of the situation, rigid opinions or even ruptures of the relationship may all occur. Nevertheless, one may hope for the gain of creating together a new perception of the world and a reinforcement of that which we call our own within a still larger area by perceiving that of the Other and coping with differences. Thus, the cognitive necessity of facing a culturally open world is just as undeniable as the fact that young adults will have to leave their family to set out on this journey. To stop, to remain still and not to move will lead to a loss of one's identity within the world. Assuming responsibility together with others for a positive construction of the world offers the simultaneous opportunity to develop one's personality and form one's identity up to the highest level.

References

Bateson, Gregory. *Ökologie des Geistes: Anthropologische, psychologische, biologische und epistemologische Perspektiven* [*Steps to an Ecology of Mind: Collected Essays in Anthropology, Psychiatry, Evolution, and Espistemology*, 1972]. Frankfurt/M.: Suhrkamp, 1985.

Buber, Martin. *Das dialogische Prinzip* (1973). Fifth edition. Heidelberg: Lambert Schneider, 1984.

Erikson, Erik H. *Identität und Lebenszyklus: Drei Aufsätze* (1959). Eighth edition. Frankfurt/M.: Suhrkamp, 1980.

Goffman, Erving. *Stigma: Über Techniken der Bewältigung beschädigter Identität* [*Stigma: Notes on the Management of Spoiled Identity*, 1963]. Frankfurt/M.: Suhrkamp, 1990.

Graf, Peter. "Wahrnehmung des Fremden als Verstehen des Eigenen: Interkulturelle Pädagogik und Konstruktivismus." In: *Migrationsforschung und Interkulturelle Studien*. Ed. Jochen Oltmer. Osnabrück: IMIS, 2002, 313-31.

------------ / Unterreitmeier, Hans. *Meister Eckhart: Zieh aus, um zurückzukehren*. Perugia: Editrice Benucci, 1992.

Hubel, David H. *Auge und Gehirn: Neurobiologie des Sehens* [*Eye, Brain, and Vision*, 1988]. Heidelberg: Spektrum, 1989.

Kramer, Kenneth Paul (with Mechthild Gawlick). *Martin Buber's I and Thou: Practicing Living Dialogue*. New York: Paulist Press, 2003.

Maturana, Humberto R. / Varela, Francisco J. *The Tree of Knowledge: The Biological Roots of Human Understanding* [*El árbol del conocimiento*, 1984]. Boston, MA: Shambhala, 1992.

Mead, George H. *Geist, Identität und Gesellschaft aus der Sicht des Sozialbehaviorismus* [*Mind, Self and Society*, 1934]. Frankfurt/M.: Suhrkamp, 1980.

Varela, Francisco J. *Kognitionswissenschaft, Kognitionstechnik: Eine Skizze aktueller Perspektiven*. Frankfurt/M.: Suhrkamp, 1990.

The English translations of Martin Buber are taken from Kramer's *Martin Buber's I and Thou* (2003), but are referenced to Buber (1973, 1984 edition); other translations are by the author. A first translation into English of the German text of this essay was made by Ms. Beate Yildirim, to whom the author would like to express his thanks.

(NOT) SO PLEASED TO MEET YOU: THE EARLY YEARS IN GERMANY

BY ELLIN BURNHAM

MY EARLY YEARS in Germany were pretty awful. There, I've said it. In fact, those years were amongst the most difficult of my life, and they prompted me to learn more about the mechanisms behind the painful experiences. Since I started teaching English courses at the University of Göttingen's language training center, I have included intercultural training, with the hope that my students could avoid the kinds of distressing interactions that I experienced.

As the eminent linguist Deborah Tannen (1986) says:

> Whether the world seems a pleasant or a hostile place is largely the result of the cumulative impression of seemingly insignificant daily encounters: dealings with shop assistants, bank clerks, bureaucratic officials, cashiers, and telephone operators. When these minor exchanges are smooth and pleasant, we feel (without thinking about it) that we are doing things right. But when they are strained, confusing, or seemingly rude, our mood can be ruined and our energy drained. We wonder what's wrong with them—or with us (11).

Although the above was not specifically written about intercultural situations, it describes something that is a problem for many people who are new to a culture: the interactions do not go smoothly, and that can contribute to a feeling that the new environment is a hostile place. Note the key word "seems".

How things *seemed* to me in my early years in Germany led to many misunderstandings, and I thought the place was rather hostile. I frequently found myself in some state of alarm: I felt shocked, hurt, angry or even frightened by something some German said or did. Some of those experiences were with shop assistants, cashiers and other people in the public sphere. But I also had some unpleasant interactions with people whom I met at private social gatherings. This essay will focus on the latter.

It was the early Nineties and I had followed a romantic interest from Washington, DC, to Göttingen, Germany. In Washington, I knew a lot of people with international careers and experience of living abroad. Several of them were or had been diplomats. These Washingtonians were able to move a conversation gently into serious topics—if their conversation partner wanted to participate—all the while staying alert to signs of discomfort in their partner that would indicate it might be time to change the subject. I relished their ability to express serious and complex opinions so tactfully, and to elicit and receive others' opinions with open curiosity and respect. The following quotation from the writings of the philosopher David Hume (1751) could well be taken to describe that atmosphere in Washington, where

> a mutual deference is affected; contempt of others disguised; attention given to each in his turn; and an easy stream of conversation maintained, without vehemence, without interruption, without eagerness for victory, and without any airs of superiority (68).

In Göttingen, hardly any of the Germans that I met had had any experience of living abroad. Nor did any of them have a significant international component in their work. Here is an often-overlooked factor in one's reaction to a new place: are the people there at all *comparable* to those one knew at home? Are their life experiences, professions and interests in any way similar? In my case, the answer was mostly no. The problems with comparisons of this sort ought to be stunningly obvious—but they often aren't—even to people who are otherwise perceptive and analytical. This comes up all the time with my students, too. They go abroad and end up living with a family that could scarcely be more dissimilar to their own. They decide to do an internship in the United States and find themselves working in some very specialized area—a casino, say. It is overwhelmingly confusing, and that on top of the language factor. It makes sorting out all the variables very difficult, especially if the person has not had any intercultural training.

It's also important to ask: is the intercultural experience perhaps taking place in the midst of a major historical national or international event which is influencing how people behave toward one another? It was the early days of the Gulf War in 1991 when I arrived in Germany. I probably should have expected tensions, but I had moved for love and I was in such a romantic state that politics didn't matter much! People's vehemence and anger caught me off guard. Was the anger somehow, even inadvertently, aimed at *me*? I don't know—probably not—but it felt like it was, and that was scary.

Here in Germany, I quickly found myself confronted with a conversation style that could almost be called the opposite of what I had found in Washington. Criticism (of the USA) was often expressed to me in the opening minutes of a conversation, sometimes only seconds after I had been introduced to someone. The delivery itself was very direct, without any kind of preliminary softeners, and it was often personalized by the use of "your country" and "you Americans" or even "you". People interrupted frequently; as a non-native speaker, it was hard for me to get a word in, or finish a sentence if I did. They defended their views to the last and dismissed what they didn't like with "That's ridiculous!" or "Nonsense". No, this was not the diplomatic corps.

I remember one incident in particular. While still standing just inside the door of my hostess's apartment, I was introduced to a woman who, after hearing my accent and learning where I was from, said, "Now that's a country I've never wanted to have anything to do with—no interest at all!" This was probably the first but not the last time that I thought, "Is this my cue to leave now, forty seconds after I arrived?" I certainly wanted to leave right then. I felt rebuffed on account of my country of origin, which had mysteriously—in my "felt" world of that moment—become a proxy for parentage, and it was something over which I had no control.

I stayed at the party nonetheless and received what felt like a barrage of direct criticism of the United States. In these early encounters, I still wasn't able to see that my negative reactions to many Germans stemmed from my upbringing in an more indirect culture. There's an eye-opening passage in Lynne Truss's book *Talk to the Hand* (2005) about the rudeness of everyday life. In the chapter titled "The Universal Eff-Off Reflex" [and lest the reader not be sure, "Eff-Off" does indeed euphemistically stand for "Fuck Off"—*Ed.*], she explains how the English find directness so offensive that they sometimes break with their usual politeness and answer back with some form of "Eff-Off":

> My suspicion is that we have to accept what very, very strange and perversely indirect people we are before we can understand where the Universal Eff-Off Reflex has come from. It is so brutally defensive, so swingeingly final, that it clearly comes, itself, out of a sense of affront and outrage. People don't expect to be spoken to directly; it is interpreted as sheer hostility (127).

Well I'm not English, but I was raised in a similarly indirect culture in New England, and, without a doubt, the German style of directness felt like hostility to me.

Returning to that party, it didn't matter whether I agreed with the criticism or not; I was overwhelmed and paralyzed by this direct, seemingly hostile type of interaction, and I couldn't react substantively to the woman's comments. As I point out to my students, while the two classic responses to a hostile situation are to flee or to fight, it can be useful to recognize that some people freeze—they go quiet, while they try to assess just what is happening, and sometimes they remain frozen, unable to respond to the situation.

When confronted by this "sheer hostility", my fear of confrontation usually prevailed and I typically froze or fled. But when I felt pushed beyond my limit, I would fight, producing my own defensive "Eff-Off Reflex". It would consist of some particularly cutting criticism of Germany. My comment would be accurate, because all those times I had backed off, I would go home to stew and plan a retort for some "next time". Whether I would actually produce my sharp comments on any given occasion was something I couldn't predict. I mostly seemed unable to choose how to react; instead, my mode of response—freeze, back off or really let 'em have it—came out of some deep, primitive place in me, triggered by strong emotions. When I did lash out, it usually left my German target bewildered at best. Not by the substance of my remark—Germans can take a lot of criticism—but by the tone, which was indeed full of pent-up anger. Occasionally, he or she was offended and fired a return salvo. Here was a dynamic of mutual offense—what a way for us each to Encounter the Other!

On the day of that party, I escaped as soon as I could without offending the hostess, who seemed to think the party was proceeding beautifully.

Let me pick up briefly on this notion of the role of the host. One of the things which left me dumbstruck at that party and others was that my German host or hostess did not "come to my rescue" when I had someone—or even a whole dinner table full of people—arguing against me. Over the years of teaching to students of many nationalities, it has become apparent to me that different cultures have very different concepts of when, if at all, a host should step in and redirect a discussion because one person is "cornered". At home on the East Coast of the USA, it would be the duty of the host to cool the conversation down if it grew too heated, or steer it into other territory if one person appeared to be isolated. When I attended these social gatherings, I had expectations of my hosts which remained largely unfulfilled, with the result that these situations felt very inhospitable to me. In my teaching I make sure to include exercises to reflect on what the host-guest relationship can mean to different people, from different cultures, in different situations.

When direct and indirect communication styles meet, the potential for trouble is large. I now see this issue as one of the more treacherous areas of intercultural communication. Of course, when I use the terms "direct" and "indirect", I am not referring to absolutes—I am speaking of relative differences in communication style. Still, that something as basic as a conversation—people speaking to one another—can cause such misunderstandings and hurt feelings, simply because of the *way* people speak, is very important for students to understand. We all think we know what a good, normal, polite conversation is—but for the most part we just know what it is for *us*.

Improving communication between speakers from direct and indirect cultures involves learning new skills and changing attitudes. For people from the more indirect cultures, learning to deal better with the more direct Other may involve developing a thicker skin while working to understand that directness *is* polite in some cultures. Juliane House (2005) says that politeness in Germany "often involves saying what one means and meaning what one says; engaging more and sooner in 'serious talk' than carefully preparing the ground with 'small talk'" (25). Understanding that directness in Germany is not hostility, but rather a way to engage someone and take them seriously, can help one become more comfortable with the early plunge into serious topics and criticism. Being more comfortable can help one express views earlier in a conversation, before freezing, fleeing, or reaching the anger flash-point and shifting into fighting mode.

For people from the more direct cultures (in my classes usually Germans and other Europeans), learning to deal better with an indirect Other may mean acquiring new ways of listening and speaking. Something my students often mention is that indirectness can be very difficult to comprehend since they haven't grown up with it, and that it causes feelings of frustration or anger. For students who can read German, one particularly helpful book is Margrith Lin-Huber's *Chinesen verstehen lernen* (2001). Although it was written for German-speakers interacting with Chinese, much of what is explained about Chinese indirectness is helpful for an understanding of Anglo-Saxon indirectness too.

Furthermore, for many Germans, directness feels "honest" and indirectness does not. But being "honest" and telling the "truth" aren't that simple. As Deborah Tannen (1986) puts it, "deciding to tell the truth leaves open the question, which of the infinite aspects of the truth to tell" (52). And she continues:

> Selecting words to speak and information to give always entails choices among vast alternatives. The accrual of the details that are chosen presents some aspects of the truth, inevitably falsifying or omitting others. It is impossible to tell the whole truth (54).

It is therefore important for students to understand that indirectness is a sort of code, a language-within-the-language, which, once you become familiar with it, communicates honestly and (usually) clearly. The Lin-Huber book decodes many examples of indirectness in a clear manner, providing insights into the emotional rationale behind the behavior.

Another thing that my German students usually feel very uncomfortable with is small talk. This is what House (2005) says: "Germans are generally less likely and less willing to engage in 'small talk'. Indicative of this is the fact that there is no equivalent German expression for 'small talk'!" (20). The students often interpret small talk to mean that the speaker is not at all interested in them; they don't necessarily see it as an ice-breaker and a way to lead into other subjects. They seldom have small talk skills, and need to be taught concretely *how to do it*. Furthermore, they need to know that in dealing with people from many cultures, they *must* "prepare the ground" for serious talk with small talk.

For people from more direct cultures, it's crucial to understand that an indirect communication style can serve as a protective shield that provides distance from difficult situations and potentially hurtful truths. In this protective role, indirectness helps people to stay calm and peaceful. However, when the shield is pierced by unexpected directness, the control mechanism can fail, and the result can be an unpleasant, offensive-defensive, verbal outburst. Or, the result can be a freeze or flee reaction. None of this contributes to good relationships. In a work setting, a person who freezes can suddenly stop functioning properly and may appear to be incompetent. A person who flees may drop contact or even pull out of a business relationship completely—especially when there are plenty of other options to choose from.

It's useful, perhaps, to think about how each of us has something akin to an imagined "insult boundary" inside him- or herself. This is the limit to how much negative "truth" we can receive, and how directly we receive it, before it crosses our personal line and becomes an insult to us.

Therefore, a key shift in attitude for people from more direct cultures is to move away from a pure "broadcast" mode of speaking to one in which they are more consciously aware of how the other may receive and interpret their words and communication style. Good intentions and "honesty" are not enough, as without intercultural training, the other person can usually only interpret the communication from his or her cultural viewpoint.

The stakes are indeed high: friendships, marriages, jobs, careers, business deals, as well as the integration of foreigners (like me!) can all be affected by our communication styles. As to my situation, things changed over time: I met different people with whom I had things in common. I (*eventually!*) got used to the direct way of expressing things and now have to be careful when I go home, lest I offend people there. Integration has been slow, measured in small increments, and not easy. Germany also appears to be changing. I don't have data on this, but my impression from the classroom is that there is a shift in communication style taking place. The acceptance of a more indirect communication style seems to be growing amongst my students—perhaps due to the many exchange programs they have participated in. I am still learning, and that is a lot more fun than being shocked, hurt, angry or frightened much of the time. Even better, when the "lights go on" for my students—when I've helped them see why some previous intercultural encounter went awry and they know how to prevent it happening again—this intercultural communication work is downright rewarding.

References

House, Juliane. *Politeness in Germany: Politeness in GERMANY?* In: *Politeness in Europe.* Ed. Leo Hickey / Miranda Stewart. Clevedon, Somerset: Multilingual Matters, 2005, 13-28.

Hume, David. *An Enquiry Concerning the Principles of Morals* (1751). Ed. J. B. Schneewind. Indianapolis, IN: Hacket Publishing, 1983.

Lin-Huber, Margrith. *Chinesen verstehen lernen: Wir—die Andern: erfolgreich kommunizieren.* Bern: Huber, 2001.

Tannen, Deborah. *That's Not What I Meant: How Conversational Style Makes or Breaks your Relations with Others* (1986). London: Virago, 1992.

Truss, Lynne. *Talk to the Hand: The Utter Bloody Rudeness of Everyday Life (or Six Good Reasons to Stay Home and Bolt the Door).* London: Profile Books, 2005.

IMAGES OF AMERICA : A PERSONAL ACCOUNT

BY RAINER BARCZAITIS

Introduction

THE FOLLOWING TEXT is not primarily of academic interest, neither was it written with primarily academic goals in mind. My reasons for writing it are twofold. First and foremost, I intend to make a small contribution to grassroots history. I was born in 1947 and grew up in Darmstadt, a medium-size city then in the American zone of occupation, some twenty miles south of Frankfurt. And even though there are many of my age group around (and it is to be hoped that we will continue to be around for a while yet), it may be of interest to read about the Fifties and about the Americans as I saw them.

Or rather, what my memory tells me I saw. I am perfectly aware of the fact that this text runs the risk of dabbling in the complex field of concepts of memory: individual, communicative, collective, cultural (see Assmann 1988). Anyway, here is how I encountered an important Other: America.

The second reason, and one which comes closer to academic discourse, is to point out how literature can shape and has in my case shaped the perceived image of America. I'll try to achieve this by looking at one literary text in particular, Ferdinand Kürnberger's novel *Der Amerikamüde* (*Disenchanted with America*) of 1855. Again, I am not going to discuss the concept of cultural memory. To do so would mean to go beyond the scope of this text.

1 What My Personal Memory Tells Me

ONE OF MY earliest memories of childhood has to do with Americans and it must go back to 1949 or 1950. One afternoon or evening, probably in late fall or early winter, as it was already getting dark, my mother and I were travelling on a bus from Darmstadt to the small village where my father taught at the local school. As we were passing through another village on the way there our bus was flagged down by uniformed men and waved to the roadside. Out from a side street came, roaring and clanking, huge metal beasts that rattled past our bus, making their way up the narrow village street. I can still hear the noise those American tanks made and see their big bulky shapes maneuvring between the small peasant houses.

There was only a very faint menace in the scene. The bus suddenly fell quiet, it is true, but my mother stayed perfectly calm, so I assumed there was no reason to be upset.

My mother was used to seeing American tanks and soldiers. Some years before, she had seen American soldiers come up the tracks in front of her parents' house on the outskirts of Darmstadt. To see them coming was, so she would often tell me, above all a relief: It meant that the war was over and the constant threat of bombing raids had come to an end. (The end of Nazism never seemed to figure very prominently.) My father's mother and sister, who lived in the city center, suffocated in the cellar of their tenement block in the big air raid about six months before the Americans came. My maternal grandparents' house was one of two in the immediate vicinity to have been destroyed by a stray blast bomb. Casualties there were none. My grandfather rebuilt the house, using mainly the old bricks with the mortar chipped off: *Ziegelsteine klopfen*, tapping bricks, was a widespread activity after the war.

Americans were a very common sight in Darmstadt in the

Fifties and Sixties. Americans mostly meant soldiers. Soldiers meant: blacks, and some whites. (This is very probably a false impression. Blacks were on the whole rare in Germany at the time; and it may well be that they have stuck in my memory more than the white soldiers.) To me, Americans seemed almost like big children—older than me, obviously, but accessible in a way that put them in a category different from the adults around me. They seemed much more easygoing and spontaneous. One evening we were stopping at a red light behind a US Army truck; soldiers were sitting on the open back under tarpaulin, black faces. They pointed up to the sky and gestured to us, grinning. My father rolled down the window and called out to them: "You mean the way to heaven?" The guys on the truck shook with laughter and gave "thumbs up"-signs. (This can't have occurred earlier than 1959, as we already owned a car, a grey secondhand VW beetle that required double declutching for downshifting. My parents had to take extra driving lessons to learn the technique.)

Another scene I clearly remember probably belongs to an earlier period, around 1955. My father took me to fly a kite in a big field, some ten minutes by bicycle from where we lived. (I would ride on a small saddle mounted on the crossbar of his bike right behind the handlebar, with my feet on small footrests beside the front wheel.) In the field there was a US Army camp. They must have been on field training—rows of tents were set on both sides of a small driveway on the forest edge. Our kite was do-it-yourself, made from newspaper sheets, which were rather coarse and heavy at the time, and it had a long tail. Too long perhaps: The kite turned out to be a dismal failure. It just would not consent to go up in the air. So in a last desperate attempt my dad got on his bike and tried to get the kite to fly by pulling it along behind him. And as there wasn't all that much room, when he got to the edge of the camp he simply went on and rode his bicycle between the tents. The tent-flaps opened and showed seemingly endless numbers of grinning faces: The soldiers (again I seem to remember mostly black faces) got out of their tents and stood cheering and laughing, literally slapping their thighs with glee at the cyclist with a big, clumsy kite spinning behind him like a ship's propeller.

Besides seeming good-natured and fond of a good joke, Americans were rich and not reluctant to share their wealth. Some five minutes' walk from our house was an American barracks with a baseball field right next to the iron fence with barbed wire on top. I never knew what the rules of that game were, but one of the players would obviously try to throw the ball past another player who held a big stick. Sometimes the stick-man would hit the ball way out into the playing field and then run like hell. At other times, not very often, the ball glanced off his round stick, rose up into the air, spun backwards over the top of a high mesh wire behind the players and fell into the street below. That was my chance: I would run after the ball—a funny kind of ball, not like ours, smallish, quite hard, and not very bouncy—and throw it back over the fence It seemed that they only had the one ball and had to wait till they got it back. Then a player would sometimes throw me a ten Pfennig coin, or two: pocket money if ever there was one! I didn't have any money of my own, pocket money not being a very well-known concept at the time, and twenty Pfennigs would buy you four sachets of sherbet powder: riches! I distinctly remember that on one occasion I even got fifty Pfennigs, and the silver coin in my hand seemed like a miracle from a fairy tale. Many years later I started to collect certain 50 Pf. mintages, probably (although I did not realize it at the time) because I had fond memories of that particular coin.

Money was scarce in our household. A car was for most of the Fifties way beyond our means, a dream. Americans had cars as a matter of course, or so it seemed. My father was a primary school teacher (they were not terribly well paid in those days) and, English being one of his subjects, he was in touch with American colleagues. One of them, a Mr. Wannemaker, drove a beautiful silver-blue Volkswagen convertible. One day he came to collect my father for a trip to Rothenburg that they had planned together with another colleague. Suddenly Dad called to me: did I want to come along? Did I want to come along! It was like a wonderful, unexpected birthday present. To ride in a car, and not just around Darmstadt, but as far as that! (The distance was about 130 miles.) Americans were magicians, coming up with unexpected car rides and not seeming to think it at all extraordinary.

Other Americans—we never knew any personally—drove big cars which seemed to take up more than one lane on the small country roads and to us looked almost like small ships. Once we were riding in the car of a friend of ours, driving on the Autobahn outside Frankfurt. It was an Alexander Lloyd, two cylinders, 600 ccm., 19 horsepower, 3.3 metres in length, one of the miniature vehicles on four wheels that Germany produced at the time (there were three-wheeler private cars as well). A Lloyd would take sixty seconds to accelerate to its top speed of 100 km/h. All of a sudden right in front of us a big American *Strassenkreuzer* drove on to the motorway from a petrol station. The friend braked hard and just managed to avoid an accident, while the American drove off unconcerned. This must have been in or around 1957. Obviously, there were other Americans, not as nice as the ones we knew, but that never really bothered us. (By the way: "Road Cruiser" is what dictionaries give for *Strassenkreuzer*, but it looks like a very German concept. To Americans it was an automobile, pure and simple.)

I don't remember ever having come across a really nasty person from the USA, personally. On the contrary, Americans were renowned for being helpful. The age of the *Care-Paket*, the American CARE aid parcels, was fondly remembered. One day my dad called me down to the cellar: Behind some other stuff on the shelves he had dug out a tin of American corn, and he told me about how they had fed on the strange and not very tasty stuff in the bad days after the war. When we opened it, it tasted extremely nasty and we threw it away. But there was another goody, a real one that CARE had introduced us to: milk powder! There were still a few containers lying around, and I used to secretly open the lid and have a spoonful or two.

So, Americans were the food aid people, even if some of the food had a funny taste. (I know today that in this particular case it was basically a linguistic mistake: German translators after the Second World War didn't realize what "corn" meant—for them it signified German *Korn* = "grain", so they welcomed it. Until people had tasted it, that is, but by then it was too late. A linguistic mistake due to a cultural gap.)

Another instance of American aid figured prominently long after it had actually happened: The Berlin Airlift. In 1948-49 we lived not far from Rhein-Main Airport and even though I was very small, I seem to remember the drone of airplanes in the sky. What I certainly remember is the term *Fliegender Güterwagen*, Flying Boxcar, the planes used in the Airlift, and I see that plane in my mind, slowly crossing in the sky overhead. There is no sense of threat that I can remember.

My parents had more personal contact with Americans in the Fifties. I remember quite well the evenings they spent with friends listening to records and talking about music. Some years later, my father told me the story of how he got to know them: One afternoon in December when it was already dark outside, there came a ring on the bell. My father opened the door (no remote control opening of doors in those days) and found himself face to face with an American soldier in uniform. When he had got over his slight uneasiness, the soldier enquired whether his information that my father taught English was correct and, if so, could he give his girl friend lessons? My father consented and was introduced to the German girl. As far as I know, the American, his name was Don, had had musical training as a pianist. He was an officer at the barracks near our house.

My parents and the American/German couple got on quite well and finding that music was a common interest led to meetings in our living room after the language lessons. I remember lying in a bed and listening to strains of piano tunes from the room. I would lie awake, because they were sitting in what doubled as my bedroom; after Don and his girl friend Flora had left I would be carried from my parents' bedroom to sleep on the couch. The musical evenings were probably the reason my parents bought their first record player. I still have Don's present to my parents for Christmas of 1957, a Wilhelm Kempff recording of two Brahms Rhapsodies, in *ffrr*—full frequency range recording. When Don and Flora married, my parents were of course invited, and they kept in contact for many years afterwards.

Not the only musical memories, those. Sometimes, trumpet calls would float on the air. It was only long after I first heard them that I realized what they were: bugle calls in the barracks, often for taking down the flag. Other audible signs of American presence may not have sounded as sweet: When the Army trucks came down the road to where they had to downshift and turn into a side street, they had a trick of deliberately making the engine misfire with a bang, and would then accelerate away with a roar. For me as a young boy, it was a sign of some technical marvel I did not comprehend but would certainly do myself when I was big. The grown-ups were not quite so pleased.

Another musical influence came with a group of American missionaries who made their appearance in the late fifties. Their slogan was "Christ for a divided Germany", and they seemed genuinely astonished when they found that there were Christians in Germany, even born-again Christians who actually shared their faith. For Americans, Germany at the time must have been the Nazi country. Tom Lehrer's song *MLF Lullaby* (1964) made me realize that when I came across it in the Seventies: "Once all the Germans were warlike and mean, / But that couldn't happen again. / We taught them a lesson in nineteen eighteen / And they've hardly bothered us since then" (Lehrer 1981, 94). The concept of the "Other" works both ways, of course.

What these American missionaries brought had not been heard of in our (very strictly pietistic) tradition of divine service: A big Hammond organ which was played in services to hymns like *Onward, Christian Soldiers*. From the mid-Fifties onwards there was an influx of Anglo-American songs and hymns from the American evangelical tradition, some translated, some with German texts set to the original tune. In those days our personal acquaintance with Americans grew, and we were introduced to some unusual concepts: A woman driving the family car just as often as the husband did was one of them. And for me, the exciting experience of a huge American fridge with big containers of ice cream—and their son, a boy of my age, being allowed to help himself! Ice cream was a treat for my family, and here it was doled out liberally to all and sundry!

2 What Others Told Me: Instances of Preconception

THIS MAY BE a good moment to stop and consider. Because, you see, in the matter of ice cream I was a bit torn. Sure, I enjoyed the treat, but wasn't it at the same time an instance of what I had constantly heard grown ups say: that Americans spoiled their children? That children were simply allowed to do as they pleased and in some cases had even become petty tyrants, with their parents not daring to contradict them?

And was not that in itself just an instance of the general distrust with which adults seemed to view "America"? America was supposed to be lacking in culture, quite generally. For me, this played itself out not least in that new kind of stuff for reading: comics. I was never allowed to read, let alone buy, Mickey Mouse or any of those other colorful, fancy magazines (not even the German substitute, Fix und Foxi). My father was actively involved in a citizens watch group called the *Jugendschriftenausschuss* who saw their goal in protecting unsuspecting youths from the menace of *Schund und Schmutz*, *i.e.*, trash (such as comics) and dirt (books considered pornographic). Comics were suspicious to say the least, and comics were American influence (at least that was how many people saw it). Good reading they most emphatically were not.

The colorful pulp magazines with their speech bubbles instead of good long sentences ("answer in a full sentence" was a typical admonition in school) were only part of the objectionable influence of America. Interestingly enough, talk was always of *America*, rather than of individual Americans. It was an influence threatening to corrupt superior cultural values—ours. I recall my father showing me a letter from a girl of about thirteen which had been published in one of the German magazines modeled on the American "culture" (I assume it must have been *Bravo*; the letter was reprinted in a brochure for *Jugendschriftenausschuss* purposes). The most dreadful sentence read: "What can Beethoven mean to us today when we have far better music, like Elvis?" This was crystal-clear proof of the noxious influence of America on the pure and deep culture of Germany.

There was more along those lines. The very colorfulness of America was deeply suspicious. When Christmas time came around, we would sometimes go and have a look at the houses in "Lincoln Village" where American soldiers, mostly officers, lived with their families. The windows were gaudy light shows, blinking horrors of red and white and blue and green, some with that most unchristian figure, Santa Claus, with his improbable herd of reindeer pulling a sleigh. It felt almost like a trip to a heathen village. It was the absolute opposite of "our" Christmas, as described by the German Romantic poet Joseph von Eichendorff: "Markt und Strassen stehn verlassen / Still erleuchtet jedes Haus…" ("deserted markets stand, and streets, / every house is quietly lit"). Nothing quiet here.

The lights also meant that money was being spent frivolously. Just like the huge cars that many Americans drove, they were simultaneously a marvel and a threat, being part of a culture of hedonism that did not fit in with the principles of thrift on which our existence was based. Thrift was a good Christian virtue, and very German. America, notwithstanding good Christians like our friends the missionaries, was after money. Time is money, knowledge is money, people are measured in terms of money. Again, this was (had I realized it at the time) a rather contradictory experience: Americans were rich and not miserly, but they were reproached for making money their god, at least that was what I heard people say.

Needless to say, the world I experienced outside of and side by side with personal friendship was a world of cliché, in many cases of prejudice. This is not the place to go into the intricacies of the research on prejudice, but the simple fact that both views could exist side by side points to the fact that "America" was to a large part the product of preconceived opinion. That does not necessarily mean it was factually wrong in every single case, but it certainly meant opinions being held without checking them against facts. As I grew older, I began to comprehend that there was a gap between my own personal experiences and the general, socially acceptable image America projected. Or should I say: that many Germans projected onto America? Where were the roots of that generalized image?

3 Ferdinand Kürnberger: Some Roots of Preconception

IT WAS AT university—I had taken German and English language and literature as my major subjects—that I stumbled upon a novel by one Ferdinand Kürnberger, an Austrian author who did not seem to play a very important role in modern literary life. What held my interest was the book's title: *Der Amerikamüde*—in English: *Disenchanted with America*. I bought the paperback, and when I had read the first fifty or so pages, I could hardly believe my eyes. Here, gathered together, were many of the preconceived ideas that I had encountered—in a book published in 1855! So did literature shape the world, after all? And who was this Kürnberger?

A very brief outline (for more detail, see any good biographical or literary reference work, *e.g.*, Killy 2010): Ferdinand Kürnberger (1821-79) was a "48er", an Austrian who took part in the revolution of 1848 and as a consequence had to flee his native Vienna for exile in Dresden, where he was incarcerated on (unfounded) charges of again taking part in revolutionary activities. Kürnberger published novellas and essays, though his life-long ambition to be recognized as a dramatic author came to nothing. But in his day and age, he became a well-known and respected figure. Karl Kraus, at least in his early years, quotes him repeatedly and approvingly; Ludwig Wittgenstein chose an aphorism of his as motto for his *Tractatus Logico-Philosophicus* (1922):

> Motto: …und alles, was man weiss, nicht bloss rauschen and brausen gehört hat, lässt sich in drei Worten sagen.—Kürnberger (21). [And everything one knows, knows and has not just heard murmuring and humming, can be expressed in three words.—Kürnberger.]

Kürnberger wrote *Der Amerikamüde* in Frankfurt, where he had found temporary political refuge (asylum is our modern word) and a publisher willing to make advance payment for a novel meant to catch the public eye. Kürnbeger hoped to put his finances on a sound basis with the book, and he was successful: *Der Amerikamüde* sold 10,000 copies, which at the time was quite an impressive figure. In terms of books sold it was to remain Kürnberger's greatest achievement on the literary market, and it was the book he became famous for. But it also meant that he was unable to pursue the career as a dramatic author that he craved, and the book was finished in some haste. Lengauer (in his Afterword to the 1985 edition) points out:

> Es kennzeichnet das zwiespältige Verhältnis des Autors zu seinem erfolgreichsten Werk, dass er sich 1878 nur mehr dunkel an den Text erinnert: Er hat ihn seit der Lektüre der Korrekturbogen nicht mehr in der Hand gehabt (565). [A mark of the ambivalent attitude the author had to his most successful work is the fact that in 1878 [when he was asked to write an updated version, which he declined to do—*R. B.*] he had only vague memories of

the text: The last time he had held it in his hands was when he read the proofs.]

There were various reasons for the book's commercial success—which has also had a consequence for our own time, as I shall explain shortly. Two important reasons are these: Kürnberger wrote a lively and vivid prose, even though the modern reader will find some passages a bit outdated and verbose, and his book was part of a larger and very topical discourse, namely books about emigration to America. Seventeen years before *Der Amerikamüde*, a book with the title *Die Europamüden* (*Disenchanted with Europe*) had been published, a modest literary success at the time and a clear backdrop to Kürnberger's book. (For the German emigration discourse as well as the relevance of America for nineteenth-century German literature in general, see: Durzak 1979; Kriegleder 1999; Gulddal 2009.)

All the same, the book might have failed commercially, had it not been for a third and probably the most important factor. At his publisher's behest, Kürnberger based the novel's central character, Karl Moorfeld, on a well-known literary figure, Nikolaus Lenau. Lenau (1802-50) was an immensely popular poet of lyrical *Weltschmerz* ("world-weariness") (he is sometimes called "The German Byron"). He had undertaken a journey to the United States in 1832, ostensibly to find new grist for his poetical mill. (At least, this was how Lenau portrayed himself. In reality he had at least equally important financial reasons for his journey—see Gulddal, 430 f., and Diner 2003, 47-9). He returned to Germany in 1833, having spent less than a year in America, and gave vent to his very unfavorable impressions. In 1853, Lenau's letters written during the journey were posthumously published. Not only did Kürnberger use their factual (or at times counter-factual) content extensively for his novel (see Schmidt-Bergmann 1990, 78 f.), in his own venture he profited immensely from the well-known conclusion of those letters: Lenau's complete and utter disappointment with America. Lenau had, because of his death only five years earlier and through the publication of his letters two years before the novel appeared, set the scene that Kürnberger used so deftly.

4 Conclusions

THE SUCCESS STORY of Kürnberger's novel has, I believe, a consequence for us today. Let me try to explain.

Kürnberger, by no means the first author to write critically about America (see Sammons 2000, 385, with more sources), had struck a note which reverberated not just in contemporary intellectual circles. Sales of 10,000 can only be accounted for by assuming a much wider readership, and the fact that he was asked to write a sequel in 1878 shows that there was a ready market for his topic. This is partly because his topic is not just anti-Americanism. His novel adopts a two-pronged approach to America: The book has a "negative" aspect in its bitter criticism of the New World; but it also has a "positive" counterpart in its idealization of everything German. The Other is, in this case, an almost mechanically constructed mirror image of what is perceived as "the Self". Supposedly German values along the lines of *Gemüt* ("depth of feeling"), *Innerlichkeit* ("inwardness"), *Geist* ("spiritual awareness"), *Kultur* ("cultural sophistication")—you name it, it's all there.

Here are just two instances of what I consider to be the book's long-lasting influence. The first extract: at a reception given in the sumptuous house of the millionaire Bennet, a figure Kürnberger introduces in a fairly favorable light, Moorfeld hears a Dr. Channing (modeled on the historical figure) talk about education in America. One of the central statements made in this scene is:

> Wo sich Trotz, Mutwillen, Starrsinn und Hang zur Widersetzlichkeit kundgibt, wird sie mit Freude begrüsst. Die Kinder üben vollkommene Überlegenheit gegen ihre Eltern (247). [Wherever defiance, mischief, stubbornness and a

tendency to disobedience make themselves felt, they are welcomed with joy. Children are in all respects their parents' superiors.]

This extract shows a clear parallel to the "Americans spoil their children" cliché referred to above. Formulated in a slightly more modern way, it could have been pronounced in my Germany of the Fifties.

The second extract focuses on German values in America. Moorfeld has watched a stage spectacle in New York that is imbued with every conceivable horror. The last sentence is "Moorfeld ergriff die Flucht" ("Moorfeld took flight", 114). The following chapter then begins:

> Als Moorfeld unter den stillen Nachthimmel heraustrat, ward ihm eine freundliche Überraschung. Deutsche Handwerker zogen am Hause vorbei und sangen eines ihrer schönsten Heimatlieder [...] wie hob sich deutsches Mass von amerikanischer Grassheit hier so sonnenhell ab! (115).
> [As Moorfeld stepped out under the quiet night sky, he met with a pleasant surprise. German artisans walking past the building chanted one of their most beautiful folk songs from back home [...] how German moderation shone, sunlike against the crass American spectacle!]

Good old German culture is vastly superior to anything American—see comics, or Christmas lighting.

Passages like this one—and there are dozens—strike today's reader as chauvinistic, to say the least. But we should not forget that texts are part of a discourse set in specific temporal, social, political circumstances. Kürnberger was a nationalist and a liberal—in the mid-nineteenth century this was by no means a contradiction in a "Germany" which actually consisted of forty-odd small or even very small territories. The *Deutsche*

Bund (German Confederation) was a loose federation of territories consisting of 39 separate entities. A nationalist in 1855 was in many ways a progressive. Nationalistic verses, songs, and broadsheets were often connected with the ideas of 1848 and of 1817, the dreaded "liberal" ideas persecuted by the authorities under the Carlsbad Decrees. It is this persecution which drove Benthal, the other central character in Kürnberger's novel, into American exile. Benthal, too, is extremely German. His utopia, with which Moorfeld agrees wholeheartedly, is as follows:

> Ganz Nordamerika wird deutsch werden, denn unsere Einwanderung stützt sich dann [*i. e.*, wenn Deutschland geeint ist] auf ein mächtiges Mutterland [...] Aber was sag ich ganz Nordamerika? Die ganze Welt wird deutsch werden [...] die Wachtposten der Kultur werden auf dem ganzen Erdenrund abgelöst und mit deutscher Mannschaft bezogen werden (203).
> [All of Northern America will become German, for our immigration will then [*i.e.*, when Germany is unified] be backed by a mighty mother country [...] But why do I say all of Northern America? The whole world will become German [...] the sentries of culture all over our earth will be relieved and replaced by German staff.]

Passages of this kind are more than liberal, idealist dreams of a unified Germany. In hindsight, even when we try and read them with the political situation of the 1850s in mind, they must be viewed as forerunners of the worst German chauvinistic excesses. But there is something else here which pertains to the historical context.

With his novel, Kürnberger was mainly out to earn money. This meant that he had to cater for a mass readership. And after the revolutionary movements of 1848 had been defeated, there was another side to nationalism, one which was not in itself progressive.

The ruling aristocracy had found it convenient to channel nationalist sentiment away from the dangerous connection with liberal ideas of constitutions and the like. Being proud of German values had become a way of distracting people from ideas of freedom. Similar techniques had worked for them during the so-called Age of Biedermeier in the 1830s: security and a modest prosperity, coupled with national pride. So what Kürnberger does in his book is play to the stereotypes he found (not least because of the Lenau story) in his audience. And by doing so in a pleasantly readable text with a thrilling story, the book could not but confirm the readers' stereotypes—or at least their expectations. Kürnberger does not analyze the foreign culture. What he does is use it as a backdrop for the affirmation of "the Self", the perceived image of German culture as it was seen, or desired. Moorfeld is the protagonist of a romantic Germany of spiritual strength; Benthal represents the romantic-nationalist ideal of a unified Germany projecting its values beyond its borders. In the 1850s, political development was on the verge of turning these ideas into aggressiveness.

In 1878 the context had changed. Now German nationalism had proved itself to be militarily aggressive. Austria had been "put in its place", France, the arch-enemy, had been beaten "in the field", and nationalistic pride was overwhelming. Kürnberger, when asked to write a sequel and bring the book up to date, quite obviously balked. He pointed out that the book belonged to a particular time. He offered to write a new preface—sadly, he never wrote it, it would have made interesting reading.

Why interesting? I think because of something that Kürnberger was aware of. Arno Schmidt, a German writer of the mid-twentieth century, put it succinctly in the case of another nineteenth-century writer, though we might almost assume that it actually was *Der Amerikamüde* that he had in mind. His author publishes

> [...] Szenen aus der Modernen Welt, alle flach und hastig gearbeitet [...] in ewiger Wiederholung [...] Er

hat sie auch zum grössten Teil flüchtig und nur des Honorariums halber verfasst [...] wenn mir ein Schriftsteller ausdrücklich versichert, er habe solches Zeug nur aus schändlicher erbarmungswürdiger Not und um des blanken Lebensunterhaltes willen hingeschrieben [...], dann weiss ich, dass ich die Ergebnisse gar nicht zu seiner Beurteilung heranziehen darf, und auch er selbst gewünscht hat, dass All das in Vergessenheit gerate, und zwar so schnell wie nur irgend möglich! (Schmidt 1958, 377 f.).

[scenes from the Modern World, all of them shallow and hastily cobbled together, in constant repetition. Most of them are, then, perfunctory productions he produced simply for money's sake. If a writer expressly declares that he wrote such stuff down for no other reason than wretched naked distress and simply to make ends meet, I know that I ought not to consider the results when appraising that author, and he himself wished to consign all that to oblivion, and as quickly as possible at that!]

Kürnberger called the work of finishing *Der Amerikamüde* for his publisher *Notzucht*—rape (Lengauer, Afterword, 572).

Passages denouncing the money-grubbing nature of Americans may well have this as their more or less conscious source. Sammons thinks this suggestion "rather overingenious" (387, footnote 7)—he is referring to Lengauer, whose suggestion it is—though Arno Schmidt, who was himself in a similar situation, seems to corroborate the assumption.

We may thus try to excuse the writer, particularly as he more or less clearly distanced himself from the book in his later years (see Sammons, 391). But what about the impact of his text?

Roughly speaking, a literary text can be regarded as an interaction between a textual substrate and a reader's set of context variables. Let us return first to the nature of the text. We said that it was easily readable and affirmative of stereotypes on the part of the reader. If we look at the typical reader of texts of this nature, we find that they have a habit of taking the text for granted in the sense that they view it not so much as an entity with its own set of context variables, but as a kind of container where they can find a plot, a story, a reality—in a word: truth. Certainly truth of a special kind—not very many will read a novel as a simple rendering of reality, although these may well exist. (I wonder how many readers will have questioned the way Moorfeld communicates effortlessly with every person he meets. Language problems are certainly among the most common that you will be faced with in a foreign culture, but not in Kürnberger.) Particularly in the kind of reader-text relation that we find in trivial texts, readers are often willing not so much to suspend disbelief as to swallow the text wholesale. This uncritical attitude, coupled with a text that affirms stereotypes, can easily lead to greater certainty on the part of the uncritical reader, so that he or she will come away with stereotypes hardened into clichés, clichés hardened into prejudices. Thus a foundation is constructed or strengthened on which more texts can build to confirm the image of the Other and affirm the image of the Self.

Jessica Gienow-Hecht (2006), in assessing Dan Diner's essay on anti-Americanism, states that "each epoch has its own forms of anti-Americanism, and it is misleading to assume, as Dan Diner does for Germany, that one and the same anti-Americanism has simply assumed different forms at different times" (1069) This is a warning that should be kept in mind. The anti-American sentiments of the 1950s are not Kürnberger's. Still, Kürnberger's novel laid down or consolidated a tradition for others to build on. It forms a strand of German cultural memory. Closer analysis might support or undermine that hypothesis. Personally, I am convinced that the attitudes to America that I experienced as socially acceptable go back at least a hundred years.

References

Assmann, Jan. "Kollektives Gedächtnis und kulturelle Identität." In: *Kultur und Gedächtnis*. Ed. Jan Assmann / Tonio Hölscher. Frankfurt/M.: Suhrkamp, 1988, 9-19.

Diner, Dan. *Feindbild Amerika: Über die Beständigkeit eines Ressentiments* (1993, as *Verkehrte Welten*). Munich: Propyläen, 2002. (English version: *America in the Eyes of the Germans: An Essay on Anti-Americanism*. Transl. Allison Brown, introduction by Sander L. Gilman. Princeton, NJ: Marcus Wiener, 1996.)

Durzak, Manfred. *Das Amerikabild in der deutschen Gegenwartsliteratur: Historische Voraussetzungen und aktuelle Beispiele*. Stuttgart: Kohlhammer, 1979.

Gienow-Hecht, Jessica C. E. (2006). "Always Blame the Americans: Anti-Americanism in Europe in the Twentieth Century." In: *American Historical Review*, 10, 2006, 1067-91.

Gulddal, Jesper. "That Most Hateful Land: Romanticism and the Birth of Modern Anti-Americanism." In: *Journal of European Studies*, 39, 2009, 419-54.

Killy Literaturlexikon: Autoren und Werke des deutschsprachigen Kulturraums. Ed. Wilhelm Kühlmann. Second edition. Berlin: de Gruyter, 2010.

Kriegleder, Wynfried. *Vorwärts in die Vergangenheit: Das Bild der USA im deutschsprachigen Roman von 1776 bis 1855*. Tübingen: Stauffenburg, 1999.

Kürnberger, Ferdinand. *Der Amerikamüde* (1855). With an afterword, notes and a chronological table by Hubert Lengauer. Berlin: Volk und Welt, 1985.

Lehrer, Tom. *Too Many Songs by Tom Lehrer with Not Enough Drawings by Ronald Searle*. New York: Pantheon, 1981.

Sammons, Jeffrey L. "Nationalist Anti-Americanism of a Prussophile Austrian: Ferdinand Kürnberger's *Der Amerikamüde* in the Context of his Career." In: *History and Literature: Essays in Honor of Karl S. Guthke*. Ed. William Collins Donahue / Scott Denham. Tübingen: Stauffenburg, 2000, 385-97.

Schmidt, Arno. *Fouqué und einige seiner Zeitgenossen* (1958). Zürich: Haffmanns, 1993.

Schmidt-Bergmann, Hansgeorg. "Über die Gegenwärtigkeit von Literatur in literarischen Werken: Leben und Werk Lenaus als Modell für Ferdinand Kürnberger, Peter Härtling und Gernot Wolfgruber." In: *Lenau-Forum: Vierteljahresschrift für vergleichende Literaturforschung*, 16, 1990, 77-84.

Wittgenstein, Ludwig. *Tractatus Logico-Philosophicus*. With an introduction by Bertrand Russell. London: Kegan Paul, Trench, Trubner, Brace, 1922. Also as website, <http://www.gutenberg.org/files/5740/5740-pdf.pdf>

The translations of Eichendorff, Kürnberger, Lengauer, and Arno Schmidt are by the author.

AMERICA: "A CITY UPON A HILL"? A PERSONAL VIEW

BY JÜRGEN EINHOFF

"AMERIKA, DU HAST es besser, als unser Kontinent, der alte" (America, you're better off than our continent, the old one) Goethe is supposed to have said. He might have been right at the time, or he might have been wrong, not having had first-hand experience. As an angry young man my own impression of America was very negative, but with personal experience of America it changed, and has undergone further changes since. You must remember that I was eight when the Second World War ended.

Goethe never travelled to America, he only knew about it from hearsay, and what he learnt at the time might have impressed him, he being the cosmopolitan citizen that he was. Our situation is different. America has come closer and for us it is easier to experience it at first-hand. My personal experiences of and feelings about America—and this is what this essay is about—have, since my childhood, had quite a number of ups and downs.

Childhood and School

MY FIRST IMPRESSIONS of America were not good. I was three years old when the Second World War began, and about five when the bombing of Germany started in earnest. My mother moved from the bomb-ravaged city of Duisburg, one of the hubs of German industry, to the safe (but remote) Lüneburg Heath, forty miles south of Hamburg, where, as an old German saying puts it, "fox and hare say good night to each other". From there I could regularly watch huge numbers of Flying Fortresses, accompanied by fighter aircraft, flying in an easterly direction, to Berlin and other destinations in the east, spreading havoc and devastation. The earth trembled under the vibrations of hundreds of engines high above us. The devastating attack on Hamburg, the enormous flames that burnt the city and killed tens of thousands of its citizens, could be seen from where we were, forty miles away. Once, a bomber with engine trouble almost hit our hamlet in the forest, with the crew bailing out only a few hundred meters above us.

Living in northern Germany, our area was part of the English zone of occupation. So we did not have any contact with Americans. We did hear, however, of CARE parcels, sent from America, being given to people in need. Out in the country where we lived there was no need for them. When I was sent to a secondary boarding school at the age of ten, I remember the yellow bread we ate, baked with American corn. School meals were dished out regularly, and sometimes consisted of noodle soup with big cubes of rancid bacon fat from America floating on top, which we used to call elephant bacon fat.

A book found in the library of my school-friend's father fascinated the two of us. It was about emigrating to America and what you could expect and what you had to do if you wanted to go West. For a time that made us dream of going to America at some later stage of our lives. The English schoolbooks we had offered somewhat more detailed information about America. They were about the discovery of America, about people like Francis Drake and the introduction of tobacco, about the Boston Tea Party and the American Revolution.

That did not mean much to me at the time, in particular because the possible relevance of this revolution for our fledgling German democracy was not adequately presented by the teachers, some of whom had previously taught in the notorious Napolas (national socialist boarding schools), where young Germans were brainwashed to comply with Hitler's image of youngsters, *i.e.*, to be as fast as greyhounds and as tough as leather.

Student Days

AS A STUDENT studying English, Politics, and Physical Education at Marburg University in the German federal state of Hesse I had my first real experiences of Americans. The American lecturer teaching American studies and literature did not make much of an impression on me. His lectures and seminars were simply boring. On my regular rail trips to Friedberg, south of Marburg, to visit friends of my mother's, I very often encountered American soldiers, whose behaviour seemed to me rather childish and extrovert. It was the time when Elvis Presley was stationed in Friedberg as a soldier but had his living quarters in Bad Nauheim. I remember seeing him driving past us in his huge car and the fuss he caused.

It was the time when John F. Kennedy was elected President of the United States, inspiring the young and the old alike with his vision of New Frontiers that were challenges not only for America but for the whole world. His idealism reverberated around the world and even made me look at America with different eyes. The Bay of Pigs disaster, when CIA-trained anti-Castro Cubans suffered a humiliating defeat after they had landed on Cuba, was not entirely Kennedy's responsibility, I assumed. His clever handling of the Cuban crisis earned him the respect of the whole world. His speech at the Brandenburg Gate, in which he proclaimed: "Ich bin ein Berliner," was enthusiastically received in Germany, but to me it sounded hollow. For me it was simply a PR stunt. My enthusiasm for Kennedy had taken somewhat of a downturn after I had learnt about his many clandestine affairs with women. America, I concluded, had two faces, an idealistic one and a dark one. Kennedy combined the two. He was a champion of the western world, and of western democracy, but he had betrayed his wife.

My world view had been shaped by my family and my experiences at high school. With my father having been killed at the end of the war, my two grandfathers became my role models; one of them a teacher and faithful partner to his wife, the other an entrepreneur, a master of his trade, with his interests very much focused on his business. They shaped my values. In the upper grade at high school I was lucky to have the headmaster of our school as a teacher of history, politics and German. He was a convinced Social Democrat and has influenced my way of thinking to a great extent. Needless to say, I developed a critical attitude to what was happening in America at that time. The situation of the blacks in the southern states shocked me, the violent protests that accompanied the enrolment of the African-American James H. Meredith at the University of Mississippi and other similar events. The Freedom March on Washington and Martin Luther King's "I Have a Dream" speech were signs of hope. However, the image of America as a racist and violent society remained. Kennedy was assassinated, on November 22nd, 1963, and so too were Martin Luther King and Kennedy's brother Robert five years later, all of them champions of the Civil Rights Movement. And although President Johnson managed to push through Congress aspects of Kennedy's civil rights and social reform agenda, which formed the core of his own vision of a Great Society, my image of America as a dangerous nation persisted. There was the escalation of the Vietnam War, when Johnson committed the first ground combat troops in 1965, and a surge of troops followed (Axelrod 2007, 225 f.). Then there was the My Lai massacre in 1968, and a powerful anti-war movement staging massive anti-war protests in the USA. In this in many ways dark era of American history, Apollo 11 and the landing of astronauts on the moon seemed to be almost the only rays of hope.

Schoolteacher and Teacher Trainer

ADMITTEDLY, MY TEACHING about America in English and Politics was very much influenced by the image I had by now formed of America. In this context, the election of Nixon to the presidency did not provide any relief. The dirty tricks revealed in the Watergate Scandal compromised him and his administration and led to his final downfall. All these events did not contribute to improving my image of America, and nor did the Nixon-Kissinger realpolitik. At that time it meant supplying arms to repressive regimes like that of the Shah of Persia, to the apartheid regime in South Africa and the Marcos regime in the Philippines. Aid was also given to the anti-democratic regimes in Argentina, Brazil and Korea as well as to the Portuguese colonial authorities in Angola. When the Marxist Allende was democratically elected president of Chile the CIA funded his opponents, cut off economic aid, and masterminded his overthrow and eventual death (Axelrod, 240). All these events did not endear me to America or make me look up to it as the beacon of liberty and democracy. Crass materialism and power seemed to have been the guiding principles. America seemed to have forgotten about its idealist side, which meant the promotion of liberty and democracy in the world, and showed its ugly, realistic face instead, focusing on power and the expansion of trade and commerce irrespective of a country's political system. In Germany, E. L. Burdick's and W. J. Lederer's book *The Ugly American* had become a recommended reader in the upper grades of high schools.

The election of Jimmy Carter to the presidency appeared to have brought an honest fellow to the top in the most powerful nation in the world. Alas, his was an ill-fated presidency. He was too vague in his political philosophy, although his policies had an idealistic touch to them. His calls for a national health-insurance program and the overhaul of the welfare system were to no avail. His attempts to redress the abuses in Chile and other states failed. The Iran hostage crisis led to his downfall. A pity that such a well-meaning person should end in this way. As a peace-broker he has made himself a good name ever since.

Enter Ronald Reagan, the champion of the conservative movement, a B-actor and great communicator. His politics emphasized the good old American values of individualism, small government, lower taxes, and unfettered free enterprise. His massive military build-up led to the demise of the Soviet Empire. His appeal to the Soviet leader at the Brandenburg Gate—"General Secretary Gorbachev, if you seek peace, if you seek prosperity for the Soviet Union and Eastern Europe, if you seek liberalization: Come here to this gate! Mr. Gorbachev, open this gate! Mr. Gorbachev, tear down this wall!" (Axelrod, 258)—turned out to be successful. Yet, it was not he but his successor, President Bush Senior, who reaped the fruits of his policies. As a German I welcomed the reunification of Germany, and had it not been for the Iran-Contra scandal I might have regarded him as an American President to be respected, mind you, not a great one, because his Manichaean worldview was too simplistic for me—here the empire of freedom, America, there the evil empire, Russia. I also had serious misgivings about his attitude to rightwing dictators like Nicaragua's Somoza. In this context, he is supposed to have said something like: "I don't mind right-wing dictators as long as they are *our* dictators."

Well, too many things seemed to be wrong with America and so my interest faded.

My focus had been on England and Ireland anyway, since I had now become married to a lady from London, whom I first met in Ireland in 1964. We have five children, all born in the Seventies. With me being the only breadwinner there was no money left for expensive trips abroad, so America remained a distant and yet to be discovered continent. The opportunity came at the end of the Eighties, when our children were no longer small and I was given the chance to go to America on a six-week in-service training course for teacher trainers, almost entirely paid for by the German Marshall Fund. The money could not have been better spent, because when I returned my image of America had changed, not completely, but in many respects. Here are some of my impressions of that memorable trip in spring, 1988.

Impressions of an Educational Trip

SIX WEEKS USA: one week in Washington, DC, 14 days in Wyoming in the West, 14 days in Rhode Island in the East and one week in Indiana in the Midwest, a jam-packed program, lectures galore, encounters galore, above all with teachers and members of the upper middle class, but also with Ordinary Joe.

What was my overall impression? So much is certain: the "typical American" does not exist! Be aware of false generalizations! The Melting Pot is a myth! Americans differ depending on where their families came from, which could be Europe, Asia, South or Central America, or they could be Native Americans. Surprisingly, the ethnic heritage cannot be overlooked. It shows in the outer appearance of people, in their behavior, their customs and their culture. For instance, the strong German influence in Wyoming astonished me. The students in one class I attended looked very German to me, and when I asked them about the origins of their families over fifty per cent turned out to have German forefathers.

As far as regions go, America possesses a great variety. Joel Garreau's book *The Nine Nations of North America* divides it into nine regions. For me, having been sent to the East and West, it was the differences between these two that struck me. The West is distinguished by enormous space: unlimited prairie, spacious fields, and seemingly endless, wide highways. The freedom of the West is not just a cliché. New England in contrast has a touch of Europe about it: a dense population, detached family houses, skyscrapers, woods. The West still has something of the flavor of the Wild West about it, the East stands for civilization and culture. The people in the West are aware of the freedom and choice they enjoy, and Rugged Individualism is their philosophy. In the East, life is more well-mannered and orderly. The Republicans are strong in the West, the Democrats in the East.

In spite of ethnic and regional differences Americans have a lot in common, the Constitution and the educational system for example, and above all the habits of every-day life: shopping, driving cars, food, drinks, and, last but not least, television. The Constitution is at the center of American political culture. The people decide what goes and what doesn't go in America. Democracy is more rooted in all fields of life than in Germany, and the democratic way of thinking seems to be more widespread. At council meetings, ordinary citizens have the right to participate fully. Before they speak they have to swear an oath on the Constitution, and then whatever they have to say is recorded in the minutes. In Germany, a council meeting is interrupted when ordinary citizens want to say something, and what they have to say may or may not be taken into consideration afterwards. "The German government distrusts its people, the Americans distrust their government." There is surely a certain amount of truth in this statement by an American professor. In schools, the tone between staff and head teacher is more democratic, considerate and friendly. In Germany, thinking in terms of hierarchy is still very common. "If two Germans meet, considerations of rank arise automatically." There is also some truth in *that* statement.

The American school has undergone quite a change since 1983. The National Commission on Excellence in Education had attested American high schools a mediocre level of performance and saw America's success on the world market jeopardized. Since then there have been big changes. Billions of dollars have been pumped into schools, and the standards of final exams have been raised.

My impression: The equipment in schools leaves nothing to be desired. Media in every classroom, video-recorders and computers wherever you look. There is no shortage of technical gadgets and they are used—to entertain students. An analysis and evaluation of what students have viewed or listened to is unusual. Even in normal lessons students remain rather passive. Lecturing is the main teaching method. "Teachers are better qualified as far as methods go in Germany." Everything is revised repeatedly at school and tested in super-simple multiple choice tests. Admittedly, American high schools are comprehensive schools. A selection does not take place. The performance level of twelfth-graders approximately corresponds to the performance level of tenth-graders in German secondary modern schools. Little effort is made to activate and motivate students, and yet their needs are met to a greater extent than the needs of students in German schools. A school with a thousand students employs four full-time counselors, to help students to solve any problems they might have at home or at school (social workers and psychologists) and to help them decide on their future careers (career advisors).

There are problems galore: Only thirty per cent of the students come from intact families, most students have only one parent to look after them. Alcohol and drug abuse—called "substance abuse"—pose real problems. Almost all upper grade students are more or less involved. Dropouts are also a problem. Up to thirty per cent of the students in big city schools leave school prematurely. Nevertheless: The counselor system could be a model for Germany

For a person coming from a provincial German town the shopping malls were a completely new experience. Every town has one or more, mostly only accessible by car. Gigantic conglomerations of buildings, surrounded by huge parking lots. They are at the center of America's glitz culture. In them, all kinds of shops are assembled, protected from wind, rain, and the cold. Music is discreetly played and a market atmosphere sends customers into ecstasies. Shopping becomes a truly pleasurable event. Opening and closing hours don't seem to exist, and even on Saturdays and Sundays shops are open until 10 p.m. Students and even teachers often take on part-time jobs in these malls to increase their pocket money or salary. Your teacher as a salesperson in a bookshop—that would be an absurd idea in

Germany. The shopping malls have become important centers of American culture, a materialistic culture that is dominated by glitzy facades and superficialities and in which people define themselves by their outer appearance and what they own. You may even ask an American how much he or she earns.

Shopping malls are mostly only accessible by car, of which the average family has two. Driving cars is, next to watching TV, a determining factor in the lives of Americans. Public transport ekes out a miserable existence. You can pass a driving test at the age of sixteen in school costing you almost next to nothing. Going on foot is frowned upon. Even the drugstore and post-office round the corner are "done" by car. Walking could even be dangerous as there are often no sidewalks for pedestrians. You fetch your food from a drive-in-restaurant, you sleep in motels. There are no limits to your idleness. As a consequence, twenty-five per cent of American youngsters and thirty per cent of the grown-ups are overweight, and quite a number of them suffer from abnormal obesity.

That is, of course, the effect of the eating and drinking habits of Americans. They love to eat and drink—and they want both quantity and quality. Finger foods are in. Fast-food restaurants dominate the street scene. Admittedly, you are served good food in them and at a decent price. You can buy any sort of hamburger. Salad bars are top. Coke on the rocks is the national drink. You can find international cuisine in small towns and big cities. Eating-out is a very important American pastime. "We are fat, lazy and hedonistic." This statement by an American governor certainly has some truth in it.

TV: In every American household the TV set is, on average, switched on for seven hours a day. You have the choice of an enormous number of channels. Who is able to cope? What is positive is that the weather channel transmits updated weather reports every half hour, the news channel constantly broadcasts updated news, and the public channel covers politics at the local level. As for the big channels: a lot of entertainment, but little information. The constant interruption of the programs for commercials is particularly annoying. News items are packed into little parcels of ninety seconds—and perhaps two minutes "for the end of the world", the professor lecturing us on American media once said. No wonder that American schools complain that students have lost their critical thinking abilities and are physically unfit.

Intellectuals, and we were exposed to quite a number of them, have a critical attitude towards this development but they don't know what to do about it. They complain about political life being driven by emotions. The personalities of candidates, their outer appearance and their capacity to appeal to the emotions of people are what decide American elections, not the issues. Intellectual analysis and debate play a minor role. They complain about the negative influence of TV on people, leading to estrangement, dulling people's minds, and making them act emotionally.

In particular, they see this influence in literature. Novels and plays lack depth, and are focused on the glitz culture, the dazzling world of shopping malls, fast-food stores and motels. They complain about the impoverishment of the language and the commercial influence on novels and plays, with the minimalist literature that this produces. Who buys long novels and who edits them? Which theater can afford more than two leading actors? The dictatorship of the box-office was also mentioned. They complain about the shallowness of life in America, the worship of money: Making a fast buck as the dominant principle, hedonism as a philosophy of life. They also complain about the change of values: the selfishness of people, their self-centered pursuits, the turning away from commonality and social commitment.

And yet. For me, America also presented itself in a positive light. In contrast to Germany (Dahrendorf: a structured society), America is still an open society, in which the individual has a high status and can go far, and in which people are friendly and tolerant. Americans are kind, open-minded, spontaneous, rarely reserved and critical. The freedom they enjoy is genuine. For many it is the road to success. Not for all of them, though. Those that fail, the sick and the unemployed are often overlooked. The have-nots in Washington squatting in front of big buildings warming themselves on the excess heat emanating from the basements are not saved by any safety net, yet many less spectacular "losers" do not fare much better. America is less organized in this respect and still has something of the atmosphere of its maiden days. There is still a lot of chaos around. Bridges and roads are in desperate need of repair. Everything seems to be bigger, the land, the mountains, the fields and lakes, the towns and buildings, the successes of people and their failures. But where there is light there is also shadow.

A New Focus on America

AS A RESULT of my educational journey I had become quite interested in America, not madly in love, but keen to get to know more about it. What I particularly liked about it was the feeling of not having constantly to fight for recognition and acceptance. Americans unlike Germans do not seem to envy your personal strong points or what you have achieved. This reminded me of what Gregory Bateson had once written about child-rearing in America and Germany: "The American child is encouraged by his parents to show off his independence." The German pattern is—according to Bateson—quite different, since "the father's dominance is much stronger and much more consistent" and the child "is dominated into a sort of heel-clicking exhibitionism which takes the place of overt submissive behavior". In contrast, "the American character exhibition is encouraged by the parent as a method of psychological weaning" (Bateson 1972, 102.). Well, that explains it all!

Professionally, my focus as teacher, teacher trainer and moderator/organiser of in-service training courses now shifted from England and Ireland to America. I was actively involved in in-service training courses about the American West, Immigration to America, Contemporary American Drama,

American Youth Culture and America in the Thirties. In my enthusiasm I published two readers on America (plus the teacher's manuals) for the Upper School about Asian-Americans (Einhoff 1997) and the American South (Einhoff 2004). Three of my various essays published in language teaching journals deal with American topics: The American West (Einhoff 1990) American Culture (Einhoff 1993) and American Literature (Einhoff 2006). No doubt, my view of America became more objective as I was able to look at it from a professional point of view. I gained more insight into the forces that have shaped American history, politics, and the economy, and have influenced its society and culture. All that has helped me to understand America better.

During the Nineties I also organized two school exchanges between our school and a high school in Iowa. They basically confirmed my former experiences in that I was impressed by the general outfit and technical equipment of schools and the very relaxed teacher-student, teacher-head teacher relationships. I noticed the important role sport played in schools. In Germany a sport lesson every day is a touchy matter. What shocked me most was a subject called "Holocaust", which students had to attend on a regular basis. I thought that such a topic would be dealt with in history lessons. This might explain the shocking experiences my students repeatedly had. They were often greeted with the Nazi salute. The local press might have been a cause, too. It hardly ever covered Germany as a topic of interest, and when it did it was usually about some neo-Nazi group having done something outrageous. The ignorance of the American students was sometimes unbelievable. My students were often asked whether Hitler was still alive or whether they had electricity or flush toilets at home, *etc*. Well, all this did not really cast a cloud over the overall positive impression the students had of America. They enjoyed the freedom, the friendliness, helpfulness and generosity of their guest-parents, the activities they were invited to, and the places of interest they were shown.

When I think of the many Americans my wife and I met

and the families I stayed with in Providence, Rhode Island, and Thermopolis, Wyoming, and the families my students stayed with in Underwood, Iowa, I cannot but praise their hospitality, generosity and kindness.

My private visits to America in the Nineties and later had both a professional and a fun aspect. My wife and I enjoyed the vast and open spaces, particularly in the West, and the beauty of the landscapes and national parks. Some seemed rather artificial to us, though: the mission stations in California, Solvang, a Danish village, Hearst Castle, Las Vegas, or London Bridge in the desert of Arizona, connecting an artificial island in the artificial Lake Havasu to the surrounding countryside. When we came to Bryce Canyon we were not sure whether it was real or not!

What particularly impressed us on our trips to Texas, New Orleans, and the East Coast was the well-documented history of America in informative, well-designed and well-equipped museums, as well as the superb art galleries. And it wasn't only the galleries in Washington, DC, New York and Boston. The Clark Museum in Williamstown, Massachusetts, is a case in point. You drive along an unobtrusive highway, the Mohawk Trail, in a westerly direction not expecting much ahead and then all of a sudden right in the middle of nowhere, in dense forests, you come across a university town with outstanding Greek-style buildings, and attached to it a fantastic modern art museum with a collection of art that many a European city would be envious of. This is America!

I remember, as a student in the Sixties, having attended a lecture on the geography of the United States. Our professor pointed out that if you wanted to understand the history of America you would have to keep two dates in mind: 1606, the year of the Jamestown settlement, from where the culture of the South developed, and 1620, the year of the Plymouth Plantation, from where the Puritan and capitalist tradition emerged. Today I think that the middle colonies—New York, New Jersey, Delaware, Pennsylvania and Maryland—are as important as

New England and the Southern colonies for an understanding of America. They stand for America's multi-culturalism, the diversity of races, religions and cultures. Jamestown, New York and Plymouth were, of course, destinations on our trips to the East Coast, to gain first-hand information about America's past. The information I was able to gather on those trips was very helpful in dealing with the history and politics of America, and its cultural differences. The East Coast is the cradle of America's democracy and the origin of its values and beliefs.

The politics of the Nineties saw a continuation of the Republicans in power. Bush Senior, Vice President under Reagan, was elected President in 1988, but had to contend with Democratic majorities in the Senate and the House. To my mind he was a decent fellow given to negotiations and compromises, but he did not achieve much. The outstanding event of his presidency was the invasion of Iraq in order to remove Iraqi invaders from Kuwait. Operation Desert Shield and Desert Storm did not unleash loud protests because they had been internationally approved of and sanctioned by the United Nations. It was a bit of a surprise when he was not re-elected, probably due to his failure to improve the American economy (Axelrod, 263).

The Democrat Bill Clinton followed him in 1992. As President he enjoyed not only the respect of the Europeans, intervening for humanitarian reasons in the Bosnian civil war and later on behalf of the people of Kosovo, who had launched a rebellion against Serbia, but also the approval of the American people, who enjoyed a period of economic prosperity. As a result he was re-elected to the presidency and would have been one of the most respected and successful Presidents had he not got mixed up in a number of sordid private affairs. On the one hand he represented the better America, but on the other, like Kennedy, its dark side as well. He has been active in humanitarian missions since his presidency, the latest in Haiti, though he is certainly paid well whenever he gives a lecture on the problems of the world —rumors speak of up to half a million dollars for one speech! His unsavory end—he just about avoided being impeached—contributed a lot to Al Gore, his Vice President, losing the election for the presidency.

Al Gore won the popular vote in America, but lost the electoral vote in Florida after the US Supreme Court, by a five to four majority, decided to bar any more manual recounts in Florida, leaving Bush the winner by 537 votes, which a recount might well have overturned (Axelrod, 269). To my mind, the idea of checks and balances, which is at the core of the American political system, had suffered a terrible blow, because most of the nine judges of the Supreme Court had been appointed either by Reagan or by Bush Senior, father of George W. Bush. Some were of the opinion that the presidency had been stolen from Al Gore. My sympathies were with him and I understood his reluctance to concede defeat.

What was to follow did not endear me to democracy American style either. I was shocked when 9/11 occurred and more than three thousand people perished. My sympathies were with the bereaved. I understood America's attack on Afghanistan to remove the Taliban regime, which had supported Osama bin Laden and al-Qaeda as the masterminds behind the attack on New York. However, Bush's reaction, saying in the manner of a Wild West hero that his soldiers would hunt Osama bin Laden down, smoke him out and capture him dead or alive, had something alarming about it. I thought that America had long ago left the era of the Wild West, the era when the gun was the law. And was Bush really serious about hunting down Osama bin Laden? Soldiers in Tora Bora, the supposed mountain hideout of Osama bin Laden, are reported to have spotted him at a distance of 800 meters and could have captured or killed him if they had not been given orders to retreat. Well, you might think, a bin Laden on the run is a better and more persuasive argument for keeping a war effort going than a dead bin Laden.

Another war, the second war with Iraq, was not long in coming. Beginning in 2002, Bush had tried to gather support for a war against Iraq with the argument that Saddam Hussein, Iraq's dictator, possessed weapons of mass destruction. When the support of the United Nations did not materialize he nevertheless pressed on and started the war with a "coalition of the willing". Germany was not among them. The military operations did not take long to be completed, but WMDs were not found and the proofs presented before the war turned out, after it, to be rather less than that. Saddam Hussein went into hiding but was eventually caught, tried by an Iraqi court, and hanged. Admittedly, Saddam Hussein had been a threat to the Middle East and to world peace in general, as Tony Blair said at a hearing about the Iraq War. However, Bush's disregard for international law and the United Nations is unacceptable. Bush's division of the nations of the world into those that are for us and those who are against us mirrors a simple mind and, together with his term "the axis of evil", for North Korea, Iran and Iraq, is reminiscent of Reagan's Manichaean world view.

My faith in the wisdom of the American people suffered a severe blow when they entrusted Bush, in my view a ridiculous figure, with a second presidency. Senator John Kerry, a highly decorated war veteran, whose war record had been subjected to a smear campaign, lost to Bush, who had spent *his* time in the National Guard. Bush even won the popular vote this time.

The bill to be footed by the American people was not long in coming. The war in Iraq turned out to be a bottomless pit financially and not only cost the Americans about eighty billion dollars a year, but also a heavy death toll. More than four thousand soldiers had been killed when Bush left office, and hundreds of thousands of Iraqi civilians. The proclaimed war objective of bringing democracy to the Middle East sounded rather hollow, when everybody assumed that the war was about oil—and there was a certain irony to the original name for the Iraq campaign, Operation Iraq Liberation, in short OIL, which was, of course, soon changed to Operation Iraq Freedom (Hiro 2010, 260)—or was partly a family vendetta by Bush to revenge his father, who had been deceived by Saddam Hussein. By the end of Bush's presidency the American economy was a shambles. A recession had hit the country, with people losing jobs and houses (foreclosures), with the car industry crumbling, with banks going bankrupt and the whole banking industry on the verge of collapse. After eight years of Bush the country had trillions of dollars worth of debts, and the gap between rich and poor had widened, with five per cent of the people owning ninety-five per cent of America's wealth. The budget had been balanced when Bush became president in 2000. I agree with Dilip Hiro when he says that "Bush did more damage to the United States than bin Laden could have imagined in his wildest dreams" (7).

Finally, in the 2008 presidential election, the American people seemed to have woken up to reality, when they overwhelmingly elected Barack Obama to be their President, "the first American President in at least forty years to convey any gravitas" (Cush 2010, in *New African*). His is not a simple mind, but a complex one. His election seems to be proof that democracy is still alive in America. He is of mixed race—his father was a Kenyan, his mother a lady from Kansas—but overcame all prejudices and obstacles and was voted in not only by African-Americans and ethnic minorities but also by white Americans. The expectations of the American people were high, probably too high to be fulfilled. After a year of his presidency he has been unable to achieve much of what he promised. His greatest achievement so far has probably been the passage of the $787 billion economic stimulus bill, which prevented the banking system and the car industry from collapsing. A repetition of the Great Depression of the Thirties was avoided! A pity the Tea Party Movement does not see it this way!

At the time of writing (March 2010) 47 million Americans are still without health insurance, the number of unemployed is still rising, although at a slower pace, house foreclosures have not been stopped altogether, and Guantanamo has not been closed. The war in Iraq has not ended yet and the war in Afghanistan has been intensified. There seems to be little hope and little change, rather, a continuation of what there was before. In his State of the Union Address in January of this year Obama acknowledged that the people seemed to have lost faith in his promises of hope and change.

A lot of the difficulties he encounters are due to the massive opposition of the Republican Party (the Party of No), whose declared aim is to let Obama fail (duel-to-the-death) irrespective of whether his policies are in the nation's interests or not. The debate about health care is a case in point. Obama has made it one of his priorities, but the opposition of the Republican Party (as well as of some members of his own party) has so far prevented any progress. For example, the recently elected senator for Massachusetts, Scott Brown, wants to derail Obama's health care reform even though it is similar to the mandatory health insurance programme he supports locally ("Obama's healthcare warning." In: *The Guardian Weekly*). Most Americans know that the way the American health care system is organized is a disgrace for a modern democracy. For example, German TV recently had a report about a middle-class American couple that had to sell their house and move into the garage of one of their children because their private health insurance was not prepared to cover the costs of the woman's cancer treatment any more.

Of course, America is the land of the free, an individualistic society, where the freedom of the individual and self-reliance are core values. These have their historic origin and justification in the struggle for independence from England and the rugged life of the early settlers. But ideas originating in the past do not always work in the present. What would have happened to the American economy if the Obama administration had not intervened and bailed out the banking system and the car industry?

America is still a center-right nation, at least ideologically, in the heads of the majority of white people. Republicans still think that the Obama presidency is only a temporary affair and that America is their country. For them individualism, low taxes, small government and unfettered free enterprise are still regarded as preconditions for a government's success, although history tells a different story. And whenever a politician like Obama tries to redress social evils on a national scale, cries of socialism and communism are heard. It is for these reasons that Americans have no social net like the Europeans in case of illness or unemployment. Unemployment benefits are not as generously granted as in Europe. America is the only industrialized democratic country that does not have a legal requirement for a worker to be entitled to a certain number of paid vacation days. Wages in the service industries are so low that very often the whole family has to contribute to the family income. Sometimes the father or mother holds down several jobs to make ends meet. About 37 per cent of single women over sixty are poor (Walshe 2010). The survival of the fittest—Social Darwinism—still seems to be a guiding principle.

And what about the vehemently and passionately fought over gun laws? They are a legacy of the past, too. They were indispensable, when the settlers needed guns to defend themselves against Indians, the French and the English. Today, the gun laws are simply outdated. Since September 11th, 2001, nearly 120,000 Americans have been killed in non-terror homicides, most of them committed with guns. What makes this society so gun-crazy?

> Murderous gunfire claims many more victims than those who are actually felled by the bullets. But all the expressions of horror at the violence and pity for the dead and those who loved them ring hollow in a society that is neither mature enough nor civilized enough to do anything about it (Herbert 2009).

What then is America today? America has become a many-faceted society. It has integrated a diversity of ethnic minorities, races, religions and cultures. Freedom and faith have been central pillars of its society (Reynolds 2009, 585). Culturally it seems to be split along party lines, with the Democrats standing for liberal values, for civil and human rights, modern gender roles and secularism and a government that helps the socially disadvantaged. The Democrats are supported by African-Americans, Hispanics, residents of the cosmopolitan areas on the east and west coast, unionized workers and the young (Martinelli 2007, 119). Traditionally they are viewed as the party of economic prosperity. The Republicans uphold traditional values. Their supporters are the traditional, religious, well-disciplined and patriotic voters, and those who oppose abortion, gay marriages and stem cell research, the evangelical Christians and the Christian Right as well as believers in creationism. They live in small towns and rural areas, in the Midwest, Mountain West and South (118). Republicans have always been linked with business, small and big, with the idea that free enterprise is at the foundation of the nation's character.

"The business of America is business," President Coolidge is supposed to have said. Indeed, America seems to be a business culture at its very core. Success in business is the most widely respected accomplishment in America. Material success was in the eyes of the Puritans a sign of God's blessing. "God is a capitalist." This was the theme of a sermon given by a preacher in Iowa in 1997 and (to my huge astonishment) he meant it literally. The close connection between religion and business makes Americans want to accumulate as much wealth as possible, yet it can also work in the opposite direction, though not always. Those who have made it in America often feel an obligation to give back to society what it has given them. They are prepared to devote part of their time and wealth to religious and charitable causes. Many elderly Americans do voluntary work. The best known philanthropists in the past were Rockefeller and Carnegie, the best known in our days are Bill and Melinda Gates and Warren Buffett.

What does the future hold for America? America will have to accept that the world has changed, that America is not the center of the world any more, that powerful rivals to its supremacy have emerged, China above all, but also India, Russia, and Brazil, and that the world has developed into a multi-polar world, in which one country cannot disregard all the others and act in egotistic self-interest. No more cowboy presidents who think they are the law! America will have to learn that the solutions of the past do not always work in the present, and that the idea of small government will have to be reconciled with the idea of big government. America has to realize that a country that is indebted to the world to the tune of trillions is on the verge of collapse. America has to be told that it is no longer acceptable that 300 million people in a world of over 6.8 billion use up twenty-five per cent of the world's energy. Obama's legislative initiatives seem to be heading in the right direction, but the Republicans do not seem to have woken up to reality yet and hang on to political recipes and solutions from the past.

Has America become "a City upon a Hill", a model for the world? It certainly used to be. Its democracy and prosperity attracted millions of people, and it was prepared to accept the "tired", the "poor", the "huddled masses yearning to breathe free", the "wretched refuse", the "homeless", the "tempest-tossed". The freedom they enjoyed in America, the wealth they amassed could not be matched anywhere in the world. For those that are still oppressed in our world, for the poverty-stricken, it is certainly still a model.

But for the world in general it is not unreservedly an object of admiration any more. "The US model is no longer the one developing countries aspire to" (Friedman 2010). And for Europeans, in particular for Germans, it cannot be a model. A German today would not say: "Amerika, du hast es besser," for the economic, social, and political reasons already mentioned above. Culturally there might be more diversity in America, in particular as far as religions go, and more tolerance of differences, and Americans are more open, friendly, and certainly more optimistic than Germans, but these advantages do not outweigh the disadvantages for the individual. The German state may be a structured one, but it is a state that gives its citizens more security in a general sense, economically and socially, and its democratic institutions seem to be less prone to manipulations than the American ones.

America, however, has always been good for surprises, and "change might still happen" once the two wars it is presently fighting and which have depleted its resources have come to an end. Maybe the words spoken by President Roosevelt on the occasion of his inauguration in 1932 will come true again: "This great nation will endure as it has endured, will revive and prosper"—and thus regain its status as a model country, even for Europeans.

References

Axelrod, Alan. *1001 Events that Made America.* Washington, DC: National Geographic, 2007.

Bateson, Gregory. *Steps to an Ecology of Mind: Collected Essays in Anthropology, Psychiatry, Evolution, and Espistemology.* New York: Ballantine Books, 1972.

Cush, Ifa Kaman. "One Year of Obama... Is the Hope Being Fulfilled?" In: *New African*, 491, January 2010, 10.

Einhoff, Jürgen. "The American West—History and Heritage." In: *Praxis*, 2, 1990, 133-43.

------------. "Der interkulturelle Ansatz—Denkanstoss für die Textaufgabe?" In: *Praxis*, 3, 1993, 248-56.

------------ (Ed.). *From a Different Shore—Voices of Asian-Americans.* Stuttgart: Klett, 1997.

------------ / Einhoff, Katharina (Eds.). *Discover... The American South.* Paderborn: Schöningh, 2004.

------------. "'It's the Culture, Stupid!': Hemingway's *The End of Something* aus kulturdidaktischer Perspektive." In: *Praxis Fremdsprachenunterricht*, 5, 2006, 15-20.

Friedman, Thomas L. "America's Instability Stirs Doubt." In: *The New York Times/Süddeutsche Zeitung*, February 8th, 2010, 2.

Herbert, Bob. "The American Way." In: *The New York Times*, April 14th, 2009, 23.

Hiro, Dilip. *After Empire: The Birth of a Multipolar World.* New York: Nation Books, 2010.

Martinelli, Alberto. *Transatlantic Divide: Comparing American and European Society.* Oxford: Oxford University

Press, 2007.

"Obama's Healthcare Warning" (unnamed author). In: *The Guardian Weekly*, January 29th-February 4th, 2010, 22.

Reynolds, David. *America, Empire of Liberty: A New History* (2009). Harmondsworth, Middx.: Penguin Books, 2010.

Walshe, Sadhbh. "Older, Poor and Female." In: *The Guardian Weekly*, February 26th-March 4th, 2010, 24.

DAYS IN THE LIFE OF AN EXPAT

BY HANS SCHMIDT

WHEN YOU ARE new in a country, you don't know how things operate. You bring along your ideas and your equipment from home, and hope that they will also be suitable for tackling everyday problems in the new country. It worked nicely enough with our summer clothes, the cutlery and crockery. But why had we transported bicycles by airfreight half way around the world? Well, I had not had time to prepare properly. The little town turned out to be quite hilly. Even the cold season was hot. And there was so much to see: the people (first of all, they were all new and strange and they all looked the same; later on, you had to be careful to recognize and greet everybody so as not to be impolite), and the scenery (tropical vegetation all year round, unusual buildings that might be shops or churches or prisons—but we had no way to tell yet).

And so much to look out for: the cars and motorbikes—and, even more urgently, the potholes and the open gutters. Some of these holes were life-threatening, they were real manholes. The potholes were not permanent, which was a blessing in disguise. They *moved*. The municipal maintenance crew could hardly keep up with them. No sooner had they thrown coral rubble into a hole and covered it with just a faint icing of bitumen, then the next hole would open up. So in three years I used the bike maybe three times, and then only in order to get to the soccer pitch on the other side of the bay, where it didn't matter whether I arrived drenched in sweat, because there was bound to be somebody else with a higher score on the body odor scale.

After a few days we started house-hunting, I bought the local paper to check the property section. Outside the store, I noticed that it was yesterday's paper. So I went back in and asked to be given the current one instead. But the cashier told me that it was quite all right, the paper only appeared three times a week. People love to read newspapers and magazines because of the lack of reading material. So little local news is reported that the date hardly matters. I had a similar experience watching television. I guess I was one of the few foreigners who regularly watched the local TV. It came on around five o'clock in the afternoon with a children's programme imported straight from Australia. I tuned in at seven o'clock for two short bulletins of world news in English and French, followed by the local news in Pidgin English. A couple of times, the news sounded all too familiar. And why was that? Because whenever the broadcasting people for some reason or another couldn't manage to produce or relay the news, they would just repeat the newscast from the day before, and nobody seemed to mind or to notice.

Sometimes it seemed unbelievable what the local people were prepared to believe. Third-rate tricksters and conmen would arrive in the country and try their luck. One of them sold wads of black paper, assuring his customers that they only had to soak the papers in a special solution for the black ink to come off and reveal 100-dollar notes. Another one showed a brick to the Prime Minister and told him that the world's largest ruby was hidden inside. Sure enough, the PM tried to get the stone, in exchange for a couple of hundred million dollars. Fortunately, this outrageous sum was more than the country's entire foreign currency reserve, and so the deal fell through.

We rented a small house, actually two, because "small house" is the local expression for toilet. We started to explore our surroundings and our surroundings encroached on us. Weeds, strange noises and odors. In case you forgot where you left the cookie packet that you had just opened, simply follow the ant trail. It taught us a lesson. We protected ourselves against intruders with fly wire and mosquito-proof doors, and we lived happily ever after. That is, until the day that my wife prepared dinner and waited a little too long before turning the oven on. We were talking and suddenly she screamed that someone was staring at her from inside the oven. True, the country is full of ghosts and spirits and black magic, but this was just *Rattus exulans* nibbling at her casserole.

One morning I took a shower, but the water was cold. You might think, since I was complaining about the heat all the time anyway, what did I really care? Well, in the morning and at night the temperature does tend to drop by about one degree centigrade, and it is nice to think that you need a shower to get warm and wash away the night's sweat. So where was the fault? I checked the boiler and the connections, but I couldn't find anything. In the end, we had to hurry off to school and to work—and what did I see outside? Or rather, what did I *not* see? What I didn't see was our brand-new gas bottle. The locals will smile at you, and they go to church at least once a week, but that doesn't mean that they would ignore such a golden opportunity as a full gas bottle that wasn't secured with a big padlock and a chain.

Another time, even fly wire wasn't enough. The intruders were getting bigger. We were burglarised one night, as they say here. Local burglars take money and electronic equipment, they love videos and CDs, but they may also empty the fridge and consume all the alcohol they can find, prompting some nasty property owners to fill whisky bottles with weed killer. My wife called the police after breakfast, but they couldn't come because they had no fuel. They have a few cars, like the other government departments, mostly donated by "big brother" Australia, but somehow it is difficult for them to find the money to pay for fuel. So we had to make our way to Police Headquarters, to report the break in. We assumed that would be the end of it. But it wasn't. One sunny morning, an unmarked pickup truck appeared in our driveway, with two well-fed men inside the cab and half-a-dozen young lads sitting in the open back. The driver introduced himself as a police officer, pointed to two young men and asked us whether we recognized the burglars. Then he asked the culprits whether they recognized the house. "Oh yes," they had done the whole street. Then he told them to say sorry to us, and off they went again. Had that been a criminal investigation? What was the purpose of the exercise? In the customary way, they should really have come and offered their apologies, together with a traditional gift of, for instance, a mat or a pig. Were we supposed to beat them up? It was highly unlikely that these young guys would have come of their own free will to return the stolen money. After all, it was the equivalent of two months' minimum wage.

You had to be on the lookout, not just for potholes and burglars. Always keep your eyes and ears open like a scavenger or a fortune hunter, or a housewife behind the Iron Curtain. Suddenly and without any advance warning (*i.e.*, advertising) some special offer or surprise import might turn up in the shops, or a new stall appear in the market with fresh lychees or mangoes (that will be sold out in no time).

The next intruders came from the job center, we thought. People could smell that we were "fob" (fresh off the boat). And so a steady stream of youngish and middle-aged ladies came knocking on our door. Some were too shy to knock and just lingered outside until we noticed them. Shyness or politeness seemed to compel them to wait until we'd ask them what they wanted. And then they'd whisper and ask whether we had a house girl yet. We sent the first applicants away because we did not want to act like neo-colonialists and let domestic staff do what we were quite capable of doing ourselves. But we also made enquiries and changed our mind. Only a scrooge-like expat would not employ a cleaner or a gardener. Expats are hired as experts because the country simply doesn't have enough skilled people (only 0.3 per cent begin tertiary education, whereas in many Western countries a third or even half the school-leavers will enter university), and one should feel an obligation to spend as much of one's salary in the country as possible. So, ease your conscience by creating a local job, and enjoy the lazy life of letting others clean up after you. Of course, we could not indulge ourselves completely. It felt awkward to be in a house with a complete stranger and let her do the menial work. And why are the adult ladies, some of them grandmothers, called "house-girls"? Why are construction laborers called "boys"? Shades of George Orwell's Newspeak!

Not that house-girls think of themselves as being at the bottom of the social ladder. On the contrary. They have a regular income; and they can work inside a nice house protected from the elements.

Our concept of a social ladder had to be revised. Bright young graduates with an overseas diploma might present ideas in a meeting on how to improve certain aspects of the country's management—only to be told off by others saying: "We are older and therefore we know better." Seniority is a striking argument.

One day I went out with a senior foreign advisor who had just recently returned to take up a high position in government. We passed three men in dark suits and he greeted one of them. When we had found a place to sit down, he told me that the guy he had greeted was the errand boy who always distributed the mail and the morning papers. I said: "Not any more, he isn't. We've just had a cabinet reshuffle, and he's our new Minister of Private Enterprise." How could that be? He certainly hadn't achieved much in the area of formal education, but apparently he was well-connected and had a certain status in the traditional social hierarchy.

At independence, the country received a Westminster-style democracy as a gift from its colonial rulers. After three decades it has turned into a kind of sports league. The spectators or voters are the so-called "grassroots", the managers are veteran politicians who have spent most of their life in the capital but (or although they, or because they) still enjoy high status on their home island by way of birth, family relations or donations. The players are the backbenchers. The teams are the political parties, though the term *party* is misleading, since most of the parties have no program and cannot be labelled left or right. Most of the new MPs soon realize that they only have a short time to make the most of their stint in parliament. They see ministers getting better pay, a government car and free housing plus travel and other allowances. So they become disgruntled and are easy prey for the leader of the opposition. Small promises will make them cross the floor and join his group. After a successful motion of distrust there will be a new cabinet. And then the game starts again.

Generally speaking, the mindsets of the local people remained a mystery to me—and *vice versa*. But is that so surprising? Growing up as they do on a remote island with no access to modern modes of communication like telephones, TV or the internet, and not even newspapers or libraries, what can they hope to learn about the rest of the world? They notice that "white people" have these items and that they don't, that "white people" can afford them and that they can't. Why is that? Some of them assume that we are simply the lucky recipients of free cargo shipments of cars and generators and other gadgets that come from some obscure source in heaven or elsewhere, and that sooner or later *they* will be the addressees. They see only the finished products of our industrial society—how are they to know that these things have to be manufactured? Or how many years it took to develop them? They don't see the European or American poor; the only "white people" they encounter are comparatively well-off. Even we achieved a big jump up the social ladder, not by our own doing, but simply because there was no "white working class" abroad. We thoroughly enjoyed it, mixing with ambassadors and ministers and feeling that we were somehow VIPs—Very Important People.

What country do you think we were in?

MY BIG FAT GREEK WORK EXPERIENCE

BY SILVIA GRIMMSMANN

IN JANUARY 2006, I finished university. Coffeeshop talks about career plans started crowding my life. What "learner type" was I? Which businesses, international companies seemed suitable? Or was I more the NGO type? What motivated me, whom did I know, how far would I go for the perfect job?

Funny: the more I discussed it, the less I really wanted a high-flown career. What did I want? I had no idea.

Then, an email reached me: "Summer job in Greece—anyone interested?" and I thought, "Why not? I've never been to Greece before!"

The deal turned out to be: serving guests in a cafeteria on Samos; the owners would help me find accommodation. After some basic research (Samos is a large island east of Athens, practically touching Turkey), dreamy fantasies enveloped me: a bit of work during the day, delicious wanderings on the beach, soliloquies on a rock watching the moon ripple on the sea…

I bought a one-way ticket with a stopover in Athens for sightseeing. The job was to begin on June 6th.

On May 29th, a call reached me from Greece. It was my future boss! "We're very sorry," he said, "but we have closed the cafeteria. There is no more work for you."

"What!" I said, "but I've already bought the ticket!"

"Sorry, that is not our problem," is basically what he answered.

Now, I had a decision to make: go to Samos with no job, no savings, no ticket home, no acquaintances let alone friends, no place to stay. Or: stay in Germany, apply for a job, and start a career. Forty-eight hours to decide.

The airplane waited especially for me. I only realized this after I was seated and it started down the runway. Otherwise, I might have been stressed. I sat beside Germans who travelled to Greece regularly. They explained Greece to me: it's just like Turkey, except with a completely different mentality. Helpful? Not really, since I had never been to Turkey, either. They told me to stay cool. Punctuality, for example, was not the Greeks' strong point. I took this as a sarcastic remark, but they were serious, as Germans usually are. I smiled politely and thanked them for the advice.

I had managed to arrange couches for my first three nights on Samos, and my first host was in Karlóvasi. In Germany, on the maps, Samos looked small enough. At the airport, I found out that Karlóvasi was on the opposite side of the island, and that Samos really is rather large. Yes, there was a bus. But when I got to the station, the last one had just left—on time. So I went on to Karlóvasi by taxi.

Xenophon, the driver, taught me the first phrase in Greek I would need: *Then milao Elleniká.* (I don't speak Greek.) He asked in broken English how long I planned on staying. I said, "I don't know." "That's good," was his response, "then you have no stress." When he heard I was looking for a job, he stopped the car and made a call from his cell-phone. He explained to me that a friend worked in a pool bar that was looking for waitresses—"a good place, don't be nervous!"—and that I could meet the manager the very next day. Hurray, everything was working out!

The job interview took place at the beach bar. The General Manager of the hotel it belonged to was a soft-spoken man in his mid-fifties wearing moccasins and a light-blue linen shirt. The *maître d'* had dark curls, a massive watch he kept glancing at, and black sunglasses. They wanted to know if I could speak

English and German. (Greek apparently didn't matter). The whole interview took five minutes. I would do the room service and share a room with a German girl in "Animation". All meals were included.

Only two suites and four junior suites were entitled to room service and a mini-bar, so there was plenty of time for me to sort forks, knives and spoons. Four arms were needed to lift and dump the tubs on the table. There were also clean glasses to be sorted onto the shelves. If you placed them neatly on the rubber liner and stacked the empty baskets according to the glasses they held, no one complained.

From the huge kitchen with a mountain of silverware, I saw the beach and the blue sky. A warm breeze blew through the open door—until the chef came and slammed it shut, "for hygienic reasons".

I stood there and listened to my new surroundings. Greeks yell. Maybe this is the case in all kitchens (this one served 500 guests), but to me, this was my first culture-shock. Waiters rushing from the restaurant calling out orders, busy cooks at their stoves, knives and pots clattering, the chef shouting at his cooks. The *maître* was loudest of all. He had a glass compartment that served as his office, but most of the time he was walking the grounds with great strides. He held his arms away from his body so that his white shirt billowed and magnified. The only time he spent in his "office" was to drink his urgent morning coffee and to smoke.

Once you speak Greek, you realize that all this aggressive shouting is actually quite harmless. But that was still a long way away.

Those first weeks I was overwhelmed by the sumptuous and wasteful beauty of this piece of earth I had stumbled upon. Sandy beaches spread into the glittering Aegean, hills with olive trees, flowers in red, orange, yellow, pink and white that crowded white houses and climbed red tiled roofs. The sunset ducked down behind the hills in a glorious show of pink. I looked at the tourists and wondered how anyone could bear to leave after only one or two weeks.

My first room service order came one day at lunch. "Silvia! Room 407. Take the plate, set it down in front of the lady, take the lid off. Don't say anything! Only *kali orexi*." (That meant *bon appétit*.) I did as the *maître* asked and carried the tray to bungalow 407. The "lady", sitting on the terrace in a bathrobe, had dyed curls and prodigious sunglasses. When I bade her *kali orexi*, she frowned her thick lips and mumbled something, possibly "thank you".

Greek *nouveaux riches* like her were the bane of the hotel personnel. Potbellied men in shorts took their thin wives in breezy beach clothes to late breakfast just before closing time. Lunch preparations were upset and special coffee orders abounded. Their children rode bicycles recklessly through the compound and left them lying randomly for people to trip over. They had tables pushed together for large groups, ordered food that wasn't on the menu and then left half of it spread on the table. Their favorite facial expression was a frown. To them, waiters were just someone else's slaves. They would let doors slam in their faces, no matter how big the trays they were carrying. But the hotel management looked forward to these guests, because they had money and were dying to spend it.

The job had its exciting and its routine moments. My working hours were 8 a.m. to 4 p.m. Clearing tables at lunch for an average of six guests was rather slow. Checking mini-bars was sometimes surprising if no one answered my knock but was standing in the room naked when I opened the door. At 4 p.m., I limped to my room, crashed onto the bed and napped. I was lucky that I didn't have to go back for dinner service like all the "normal" waiters. After my nap, there was ample time to go to the beach. Hotel guests left it at around 6 p.m., just when the sun was beginning to cool. Sometimes I would go for a swim, sometimes I would just lie on the warm sand, listening to the soft sea and soaking up the Mediterranean sun. That was life at its best.

My roommate was a gorgeous blonde who walked like a dock worker, prowled the grounds at night and was hysterically afraid of intimacy. I was asked once whether she had been in bed on a certain night when a large sum of money was stolen. I said yes, she was, but there were so many rumors, and her communicative behavior was so erratic, that it seemed best for everyone, especially for her, when she was sent home on medical grounds. She had knocked out two of her teeth at two in the morning (stumbling and falling over a bicycle).

After that, I was relieved to be moved to a room all to myself. I didn't care that it was under one of the bungalows, and had only one narrow window and rough white-washed walls. It was quiet, cool and large. They even brought me a TV! The hint of moisture and the musty smell could be dispelled by opening the door and the window at the same time. Privacy was maintained, because the entrance was tucked behind a stairway and the guests never suspected that anyone was living underneath them.

The language barrier prevented me from talking much with my colleagues. One day, I met George, who spoke fluent American English. He had gone to college in the USA and had come back to open his own water-sports shop close to the hotel. Nice people of various backgrounds met there, drank *café frappé* and chatted to Anastasia, the hired helper, and watched tourists fall off surf-boards. George was a particularly fine specimen of Greek male egotism. (Remember: *ego* is Greek for *I*.) He wore nothing but reflecting sunglasses and bathing trunks and had a grin that could charm the scales off a fish.

Anastasia's husband worried about her working there, which was nothing but machismo, of course. But in this case, there really was cause for concern, considering George's habit of summertime philandering. He had beach beauties lined up at his beck and call. They all thought they were "the special one". The sad thing (or admirable, depending on your point of view) was that he *did* have a special woman. She had come all the way from the Netherlands to be with him, with his consent. She was a tough, buxom blonde who spoke fluent Greek and was anything but naïve. But she stayed, because she loved him.

George's place, apart from teaching me some valuable

lessons, had a special meeting in store for me. In August, George's cousin came from Athens, as he did every summer, and worked for him. This cousin had long dark curls, a complicated name, and didn't take himself too seriously. He was shy and funny and brushed unruly curls from his eyes whenever he forgot a word in English. He lived in a house on a hill overlooking the marina. Beyond that, the glittering sea spread away in the daytime. At night, the stars arched a sparkling blanket from fingertip to fingertip if you spread your arms.

Patroklos was his name. He embodied a different, though still very Greek, type of male. He lived with the seasons, summer catapulting him out of Athens and onto the island, throwing him into the water and out into the hills. A shirt was worn only in the evening. Artwork of broken mirrors, window frames and clashing colors filled the house. He was anarchic and anti-religious. If his boss at a restaurant treated him badly, he would pick a fight and go somewhere else. His serving career had started at the age of eight, when he accompanied a crazy captain and his pet goats on a boat and handed out sliced watermelons and ouzo to Scandinavian tourists.

Winter swallowed him and locked him indoors in the moloch of Athens. He then grew quiet, pensive and melancholic. He read books and worked on his jewelry. He wore shoes, a coat and even a shawl. His curls lost their reddened edges.

Before I linked my intermediate future to this wild boy and followed him to Athens (to meet his monster of a mother), the summer on Samos had to be brought to a close. People with a contract at the hotel knew when that would be and could plan ahead. I didn't. (That was why I was hurried off to a remote conference center when the bush telegraph spread the news that tax investigators were on their way.)

Working conditions didn't exactly deteriorate, but the assumption was that extrinsic motivation was not necessary. We all ran on reserves. Stress was compensated for by yelling, smoking in the rest-rooms, fighting over serving utensils (espresso spoons were bunkered in cupboards and drawers), and delving into the breakfast buffet when it was cleared at 11 a.m. Burns, inflamed muscles and swollen feet were ignored until the end of the season.

A new girl came to share my basement, a dark-haired girl from Alsace. She did her job conscientiously. After a few weeks, she was lifelessly pale and limped miserably. But she took two or three showers a day and dressed up to go out after work, no matter whether it was 11 p.m. or 2 a.m. Like a zombie, I couldn't help thinking.

I was infected by the anarchic Patroklos and started not taking my job too seriously. Beautiful outings played their part in weakening my loyalty to a boss who never spoke to me apart from staccato commands: "Silvia! Get flowers at the reception! Put aspirin and bring them to 206!" I had never heard of flowers needing aspirin. I didn't know where the vases were, either. I had learned not to ask "why".

Employing the same style of communication that I had become accustomed to, I walked up to the *maître*'s office one day and announced, "Next week, I finish." Shaking the ashes off his cigarette, and without looking up, he said, "Okay."

I left the island by boat with Patroklos and his yellow dog Tritonas, for a cool welcome in Athens some fifteen hours later. Patroklos moved into an apartment that belonged to his grandmother. His mother and sister had cleaned it for him, and without wanting to, for me also. Grudgingly, we were given a second key. When I found out that his mother also had a key and intended to use it at her discretion, I was subjected to my first screaming-attack. Who was I, with my two bags? Did I have no family, no shame!? She accused me of living off Patroklos' wealth. It had never occurred to me that he might possess anything. In the course of events, he was indeed disinherited of the bit of real-estate that the family owned. (He was probably hoisted back onto the throne after I left.) She commanded me to leave, to go back to my "Nazi country", or else she would call the police. Patroklos took this in stride when, still under shock, I told him about it. He hadn't expected anything different. But I panicked, and my heart raced every time I heard steps or voices in the hallway.

I had to find a job, to prove her wrong, to get out of the house, and to occupy my mind. One job ad from an incentive and events agency required German, English and computer skills. I was invited to an interview and took the bus to Halandri. They needed someone to handle the correspondence with German partners, visit potential five-star locations, and accompany the groups when they arrived. Increasing salary, responsibility and a contract with health insurance were promised (orally). It turned out that the interviewer was "best friends" with the General Manager of the hotel on Samos. To prove it, he called him then and there. "Kostas, *filé mou!*"

Around this time, I started learning Greek in earnest. I studied chapter after chapter and copied the alphabet until I knew it by heart. "The dog bounded through the hills and forest of Illissia": I translated the English vocabulary into Greek and back again. I spoke the words out loud to get used to the accents, which cannot be pronounced strongly enough.

Learning advanced in waves. Some days I would plow ahead. On others, I was sick of anything remotely Hellenic. Often enough, my language lessons consisted of riding the bus and looking out the window, reading signs and ads. How proud I was when I could not only decipher ΕΠΑΦΗ (*epafi*, "contact") and ΕΦΑΚΕΣ (*efakes*, "lenses", also "lentils"), but also got what it meant because I knew each word separately! Other pieces of the disconcerting Greek puzzle started to fall into place, the yelling for example. Neither men nor women were shy about using the highest decibels their vocal organs were capable of. The person addressed could be next to them or on the far side of a four-lane highway. If the latter was the case and *you* were next to the person shouting, you flinched, to put it mildly. It sounded like a curse or a death threat—until you understood what they were saying. I was beginning to peek behind the curtain, and I discovered that the shouting was never (or hardly ever) meant to be hateful. Women for example argued over whose recipe for *dolmades* was the best. Men chatted about whom they had met the other day at the *Kafenion*.

Behind the curtain, I also found out that not all Greeks were philosophers. Athenians were simple people. They went to the market and bought fruit and vegetables for the whole week so they wouldn't have to buy them in the sterile supermarkets. They read obituary notices stapled to lamp-posts and remembered the deceased while waiting for the bus. Old men sat in the *Kafenion* with their worry-beads. Young men dressed sharply and took their girl-friends for rides and for coffee in Glyfada. Conversations among younger Athenians were about cell-phones and their extra features, about movies, or accessories they had or wanted. Philosophy etc. had happened, sure. Of course Greece was the cradle of democracy and European culture. But today, their world encompassed their immediate friends and family and the objects that they owned.

Regarding the job (which I got), I was naïve—with hindsight. At the time, I had yet to learn that Greeks are extremely charming when they want something. The form my new boss, Spiros, promised to fill out to legalize my stay and permit me to work slipped to the bottom of the pile. My pay was undermined with arguments like "That evening tasting the menu doesn't count as work" or "You accompanied me to the site for four hours, but you didn't actually *do* anything productive all evening." He never trusted me with an office key. There was a printer, but I wasn't allowed to use it, because it was too expensive to replace the toner cartridge. I had to run to the nearest print shop every time. Although Spiros was aware that I could read and write in several languages, he re-read and rephrased every single email that I wrote. This took up many hours. He also dictated what he wanted me to say on the phone.

What I learned was that Greeks don't trust anyone except their mother, while at the same time basing all business interaction on the concept of personal trust.

Another pillar of business culture was loyalty, which was owed unconditionally to your boss. At least I think that's what the following episode was about.

A German partner agency sent a junior employee, Carolin, to Athens with the client for a pre-visit. The client was preparing an incentive for a large financial consulting company. She became increasingly appalled at the lack of detail and preparation and didn't hesitate to express her dissatisfaction. Poor Carolin was stuck in the middle and turned to us in a moment of desparation. We were in a restaurant that hadn't opened for the season, since it was only March. We were listening to the manager promise us anything we wanted. The client saw the empty rooms and the unswept floors and complained. Out of her depth, Carolin turned to Spiros and cried, "I thought you had handled all this!" This is not what a Greek man wants to happen to him: to be accused of a mistake by a woman, in front of other women. His ego alarm goes off at full blast and he fights back viciously. For the moment, Spiros played it cool. He took Carolin to one side and said quietly: not in front of the client!

Back at the office, though, there was no end to the disappointed, bitter complaining about Carolin. I tried to say something emollient: "She's young and inexperienced. This is her first time in Greece..." The full blast of his wrath was then turned upon me. His lips shook, he screamed at me. How could I take sides with that witch, how could I be of help to him if I didn't support him in a crisis!?

Immersion in the host culture took its course. I started speaking Greek with Patroklos. First, he laughed at me. I tried again, and soon I could produce whole sentences that were understood and could be answered effectively. Although I couldn't follow the news on TV, commercials were helpful. They were repeated, short and offered visual support. Most movies were from Hollywood, so I could watch them in English and read the Greek subtitles. Listening was a major part of the learning process. I heard Greek riding the bus, at the market, and listening to Spiros on the phone.

I heard how sweetly charming he was to the banquet manager at the five-star hotel that he wanted to do some catering for us, how he reminded people whom he hadn't actually spoken to for a long time of the very special and successful relationship that they had. The talks he had with subcontractors were revealing. For example, we had to book yachts for a group coming in June. We had already booked two yachts, but we would need a third one due to security regulations (because of the limited number of life vests on each boat). Spiros contacted a third captain. Then, he set the deadline for the client to accept the offer so early that he was practically "forced" to raise the price after the deadline had passed. To the client, this was "due to high demand in the main tourist season". I heard Spiros speak with the captain in Greek and offer him half of the price increase, which was fair, since he had landed the coup on his own.

The Germans who came were not so naïve as to believe that the Greeks were dealing with them fairly. They were particularly suspicious of the effusive politeness, the friendliness and the compliments. But they never really knew how and when exactly they were being cheated. We emailed them detailed Excel spreadsheets of every single expense: the bus rides and the surcharge after midnight, the escorts, entrance fees, menus and drinks. All very transparent. Our international partners probably never suspected that Spiros was even cheating his own employees.

The escorts were middle-aged women, most of them English, who had gotten stuck in Greece a decade or more ago. They had fallen in love with a young Greek, married and had children. And that's when the trap had closed, since it was illegal to take your own children out of the country without the father's consent. So they stayed. They earned some money by escorting groups from the airport to the hotel or showing the way from the bus to the cruise ship in Piraeus. They were sweet, caring women who had aged prematurely. Their eyes were tired, their skin wrinkled, and their blonde hair was wirey. Between bus transfers, we exchanged thoughts and experiences. They had all worked for Spiros before and reported late pay, unreliable information about working hours and general machismo. Finally someone I could talk to! They listened intently, leaning forward as their eyes widened in worry, and counselled me unanimously to "get out!", especially when I hinted at the negative turn my relationship was taking.

When my second group arrived in May, I made up my mind to do just that. The last straw was a jaunty slap on my backside from Spiros in ebullient mood. When I told the escorts about my decision, they sighed in relief and sat back in their chairs.

I didn't breathe a word at work. I waited for the end of the month to get paid. Every day, I took home a single item, a cup or a pencil, that belonged to me. It took Spiros seven excruciatingly long days to calculate how much I had earned in the course of the month. On the afternoon of day seven, he called me into his office and paid me 750 Euros. This time, I didn't argue. He said, "Tomorrow at ten?" I said, "No problem", looked him in the eye, and left.

The next morning, I switched off my cell-phone and slept in.

To get a perspective on things, I packed a bag and hopped a few islands. Somewhere between pine-trees sloping into a turquoise sea and a frapuccino at a lonely beach café, I decided to call the General Manager at the hotel on Samos and ask if I could come back. At least I knew how things were done there. I had had enough surprises for a while. He and the *maître* said I should come as soon as possible, but I would have to stay the whole season this time.

I took the overnight ferry. I was welcomed with hugs by the *maître* and the General Manager, who said, "You've lost weight. Go get some breakfast." Later, he asked, "So how was it working for Spiros?" I said, "Well, it wasn't quite what I expected." Referring to his own experiences with Spiros on Crete, he said, "Spiros asks a lot but gives little."

I shared a room with a temperamental Rumanian girl who spoke fluent German. She worked at night, I worked in the daytime. I was thankful that everyone left me alone. I was never asked to stay late, and I was paid on time and at exactly the rate agreed. I kept my tips and was given a bonus in August.

Patroklos came after a few weeks, but I hadn't missed his dramatics.

My Greek surprised almost everyone. This summer, I learned much more about the people I worked with. For example, that they were all related to each other. Kostas, who drove the pick-up with the garbage, was the father of Angeliki in accounting, and was married to Thassoula, one of the cleaning ladies. Waiters were married to each other, a cook to a cleaning lady, the front desk manager to the *maître*. Whole families lived off the hotel. They worked hard all summer and sighed in relief when the tourists left the island more or less as it had been.

The mornings were getting cooler when I changed jobs. I was placed at the reception desk and actually given a signed contract (it was more difficult to hide me now). The reception area and lobby were clean, quiet and air-conditioned. I checked in tired and cranky guests, checked them out tanned and happy, and gained weight.

The season ended for me at the beginning of October when Katerina, the front desk manager, informed me one afternoon, "Tomorrow is your last day."

Feeling that I needed to invest some energy in my own future and that my time in Greece was coming to a close, I started spending time in the internet café, researching job offers and sending off applications. Mid-October, I received the offer of a job in Germany—with a tariffed salary, social insurance and a contract!

When I left Greece in time to spend Christmas in Germany, I hadn't seen all that there was to see. I hadn't been to Meteora or to Corinth. I hadn't taken the boat from Samos to Turkey, although it was so close. My own lethargy and my chaotic boy-friend and his jealousy had kept me from making friends and touring the sights. But I had certainly plunged into Greek culture, and bravely stood up to whatever Greece could throw at me.

Greeks experience all this too, of course: the yelling, the stress and hard work in summer, the screaming mothers-in-law, the bad bosses. But they do one thing differently. They never lose touch with their best insurance system: their family. No matter how much they may criticize each other when out of earshot—in the moment of need, they know they can depend on each other.

Traveling allows you to compare. Sometimes you find out that home isn't such a bad place after all and that you have been more thoroughly programmed by your own culture than you would have cared to admit before.

My hunger for adventure was quenched for a year or so. My German colleagues were gentle-mannered and lacked temperament. No one yelled: we spoke quietly and sensibly to each other. I had my own computer and received all the office materials that I needed. My pay came regularly, and without my having to ask for it. German working conditions allowed me to catch my breath.

THE WANDERING FOREIGNER AND A CONFLICT OF CULTURES

BY MAYURI ODEDRA-STRAUB

WHEN I MEET new people they often ask me which country I come from. This is often a difficult question for me to answer. I was born in Kenya, but I am of Indian origin and a non-strict Hindu. Until recently most of my extended family on my father's side lived in Kenya, for almost a hundred years. My mother was born in Tanzania, with her side of the family still living there. I was a Kenyan citizen until 2003, when I took German citizenship for practical reasons.

A few years ago, whenever I told people that I was Kenyan they would say: "But you are not as black as people in Kenya are supposed to be." Now that I am married to a German and have German citizenship, whenever I mention that I am German people say that I am "not white enough". When I went to live in India and told people there that I was Indian, they would laugh and say: "You might be colored like us, but you are not a true Indian." In Japan I could sometimes get by by saying that I was from India, but things would get complicated when people then asked me which part of India that might be. My forefathers were actually from a village close to Porbander in Gujarat (the place where Mahatma Gandhi was born).

Although my siblings and I were brought up in Kenya more or less in an Indian cultural context, I don't know a lot about

Hinduism, I can't read or write any of the Indian languages (although I can understand a few) and I have never returned to my roots. I was exposed to both traditional Indian and African culture, as well as to the British culture that was introduced into Kenya during colonial times. In Kenya, the modern and the traditional existed side by side without much of a problem. In fact, we took the best from all three cultures and organized our lives accordingly.

I was educated in Kenya, and then sent off to England for graduate studies, because that was a prestigious thing to do. After a decade of studying and working in London, I got married to a German and went to work in Singapore. After a short stint there, I moved to Germany, then on to India, then again to Germany, then to Japan, and now again Germany.

So what, in terms of national or cultural identity, does that make me? Where do I belong? Where am I at home? Am I an "international citizen", if there is such a thing? If these questions still matter in this day and age, then I have to say that they are really difficult for me to answer. I don't feel that I have a national or cultural identity or a home-base anymore, and maybe I have become multicultural—or *multi-kulti*, as the Germans say. I feel as though I am "in transit" all the time. Maybe the nomadic or gypsy blood that I have in my veins plays a role in my lack of a need, or the ability, to establish roots; my forefathers are said to have migrated from Persia to India centuries ago.

What I would like to do in this article is describe the main "problem areas" (at least for me) that I have experienced in the different cultures that I have lived in. It often happened that there was a conflict between what at the time seemed to be right, or better, and what I had known or done before. The topics are in alphabetical order, not in order of importance.

Attitude and Openness

I FEEL THAT people's attitude, their behavior, their openness or their directness is an issue in many cultures. The Indians for instance would want to know your life history in the first few minutes of your encounter. Are you married? What does your husband (your father) do for a living? How much do you earn? Why aren't you married? How many children do you have? And so on. This is not considered to be "nosiness"; it is a polite way of breaking the ice when you meet someone new (and also a way of discovering people's social status). I once asked a British colleague how his children were and he in return asked me whether I knew them. How strange of me—from his point of view—to be inquiring about someone I didn't know and had never met!

The Indians, Africans and Japanese have a problem with the use of the word "no". In order not to "upset" anyone or sound negative, they will often beat around the bush rather than plucking up the courage to say "No, I can't do it" or "No, I can't come on that day", whereas someone German or British would be frank (open? rude?) and speak their mind. I recently called a neighbor to ask him something and his first sentence was that he couldn't talk to me as he was late for an appointment. I was shocked and upset by his reaction. I suppose that he was just being frank, but such openness or directness still has the power to shock me. If I had been in his shoes, I would probably have talked for a while and then politely informed the caller that I didn't really have the time to talk then. What it always comes down to is the question of whether this culture of being open and honest is good or whether it is better to be polite even when it doesn't suit you.

The Asian inability to say "no" also influences my intercultural marriage. My husband often wants a "yes" or "no" answer and I often have difficulties answering in this manner. In fact, my answers are usually "maybe" or "it depends on this (or on that)" (*i.e.*, my response is conditional), which does tend to annoy him! Is this a weakness of my cultural background, where there is no clarity, or is it because people from Asian or African cultures often try to please others—not wanting to contradict or upset anyone—rather than putting themselves in the foreground?

Another point that I'd like to address here is the attitude or behavior of people towards foreigners. A disabled man who was collecting money for charity in Stuttgart once asked me, after I had given him some money, whether I had no soap at home? Was that dirt on my skin, which I perhaps couldn't afford to wash off, he inquired? I was stupid enough not to demand my money back! I have had similar encounters with couriers. One was so shocked when I opened our front door that in order to allow him to recover I had to inform him that I was only the *Putzfrau* (cleaner), and not the owner of the house, but that I could sign for Frau Straub. Another courier told me when I opened the front door: "You are living in a nice big house. You people usually live in a *Wohnbude* [*Ed.*: hard to translate—dump? hut? shack?—but patronizing, if not downright offensive]". Can you call this a cultural attitude towards foreigners, or is it plain racism? Is it the attitude of a "superior race"? Such attitudes are not confined to Caucasians. In Kenya, we Indians always thought of ourselves as being better off than the Africans (and the British considered themselves superior to both of us).

The (Chinese) Singaporeans also have an attitude problem, I would say, often coming across as big-headed, rude and arrogant. Perhaps Singaporeans feel that, because their country has now made it to developed-world status, they can therefore allow themselves to behave in such a manner. In fact, the *kyasu* attitude, where you are encouraged to think of yourself first (something very un-Asian), is highly pronounced in Singaporean society. Such an attitude may have helped the country to develop faster, but it is hard to expect newcomers to be appreciative of such selfishness, where people push themselves forward all the time, whether it is in jumping the queue to get to something first, in their behavior towards their classmates, or just in piling up their plates at a buffet in case the food should run out.

Maybe this is partly paranoia, but I find myself working very hard to keep up an "appearance"—one which would not allow anyone to point a finger and say: yes, this is how foreigners are. I have spent most of my time in Germany in the south, in Swabia, where stairways and streets have to be cleaned on Saturdays (*Kehrwoche*). I always complied with this man-made rule, whereas my neighbors would be less bothered. I go out of my way—to my family's annoyance—to keep my house spick and span so that no one has the chance to complain about messy foreigners.

Maybe the "age issue" doesn't quite fit under this heading, but I would nevertheless like to mention it here. I find it amusing how the Germans mention age everywhere, next to a person's name, in the newspapers, on TV, and so on. Your age is part of you and people have the right to know how old you are, whether you like it or not. Many cultures consider it impolite to ask someone's age, but in Germany this doesn't seem to be a problem. The Indians on the other hand try to hide or fiddle with their own or someone else's age. The age of a Japanese is the most difficult thing to find out. No one wants to talk about their age and people go out of their way to hide it. And, since they are "healthy people", you can't just look at a person and guess how old they are. A Japanese friend of mine looks between fifty and sixty but her mother is nearing a hundred, and in her mother's young days she couldn't possibly have had a child when she was forty! Usually, the Japanese don't even celebrate birthdays; only when people turn seventy, eighty, ninety or a hundred is there some kind of a celebration. For children, it is mainly the third, fifth and seventh birthdays that are celebrated with a lot of pomp and ceremony.

Children

RAISING TEENAGE CHILDREN in an intercultural environment, in a culture of iPod and Facebook, is going to be a challenge for any parent. The particular dilemma that I face is, do I raise my children in the way that I was raised, in a strict environment, or do I allow them to adjust to the different cultures that they face—in effect, a new culture every few years? As a child, I had to help with the various household chores. We had to show respect to our elders. We had to address people respectfully as brother, sister, uncle, aunt, grandma or grandpa, even when they weren't actually related to us. You didn't dare call people older than yourself by their name, as is quite normal in the West. You didn't argue with your elders (they always knew best). You usually did what you were told. You didn't wear skimpy clothes in front of older people, as a sign of respect. You were nice to people you disliked, and so on. My children don't subscribe to much of this, as it is not a "cool" thing to do. Will this make them "better" adults and influence their sense of identity or their self-confidence? Will they "suffer" because of their lack of "respect" for others? Or—will they at some point (I hope) learn to balance the different cultures that they are exposed to, as I have done, acting and behaving differently in different cultures?

In the West, puberty is generally blamed for children's difficult behavior, by parents, society and even by the children themselves. This phase can last for years (in my daughter's case, it has lasted for six years now!). But is it really puberty which should be blamed, or rather the society in which we live, the poor job we do in raising our kids, or the self-discipline that we fail to engrain in them? In the African and Asian cultures that I know, when children reach adolescence they are then considered to be "grown up", and they become involved in appropriate adult activities: hunting, helping in the household, being married off, earning a living, *etc.* In other words, at this age (young) kids grow up and take on responsibilities, rather than shedding them because of something called "puberty", as happens in the West.

Discipline

A COUNTRY FROM which one can learn a lot about discipline is Japan. The discipline of Japanese people is unrivaled: the discipline with which they travel in packed trains, with which they remove their shoes everywhere, with which they prepare and serve food and tea, with which rituals are observed, with which public spaces are kept clean, with which elders are respected, and so on. Another country which would come high in the rankings for discipline is Germany, where people love rules and regulations, keep time carefully, and are usually happy to obey the law.

Compared with this, the indiscipline in Kenya and India comes as a shock. In fact, it wouldn't be far off the mark to say that discipline doesn't really exist in these countries. Breaking the law or the rules is a thing you do, and you are regarded as stupid if you don't. Time-keeping doesn't exist; people come late even for important meetings. Indians only bother to keep time when they are getting married, to comply with the carefully calculated auspicious time of union. People in these countries throw garbage where and when they feel like it. They will keep their own houses clean, but throw the rubbish over the compound wall (those who are privileged to have one), so that it becomes someone else's problem and not theirs. When they feel the need, people will spit or answer "calls of nature" wherever they happen to be, without any shame. To stop some of these habits, people in India have started putting up pictures of gods on the outer walls of houses or along common staircases so as to discourage others from peeing or spitting against them.

Dress

IN COUNTRIES LIKE Kenya or India you wear your "Sunday best" (full of glitter in India) at the weekend, when visiting or when you "go out". People take a lot of care in their dress and how they look. The Japanese (both men and women) are also very well dressed, though they are more brand conscious than people elsewhere. The clothes you wear in Japan have to be branded, whether you can afford it or not. Many buy clothes and branded goods (a Louis Vuitton handbag is a must) on credit, and when they get into payment difficulties they would almost prefer to commit suicide than rethink their attitude to shopping!

Compared to these countries, it is really a bit sad (in

my opinion) to see how little care the majority of people in Germany, Britain or Singapore—including those who can afford to buy really good clothes—take with their dress. That applies to casual clothing, too, which is usually rather drab. I often feel "over-dressed" in these countries, even when I am doing my best to fit in. Recently, the son of a friend of mine had his First Communion (an event which is an important social ritual in Germany), and his mother wore a teeshirt and jeans to the church! The other cultures that I know would have been shocked to see that. So—what do you do? Do you try to keep up your own style of dressing, living up to your own standards of looking decent (even though it may make you look out of place), or do you try to fit into the culture and perhaps not pay much attention to your clothes?

Emotions

ANOTHER AREA IN which we see differences in cultures is in the matter of emotions. The Africans (we could see this during the recent Football World Championships in South Africa) and Indians often behave very emotionally, and will show their emotions in public. There is nothing wrong in people crying (men, too!) in public, because of sorrow, joy or happiness. There is nothing wrong in being loud or excited. Such emotions are generally suppressed in countries like Germany and Britain. But worse still in this respect are the Japanese—again, this is something very un-Asian—who don't show *any* emotions in public, in order not to "burden" others. A very good Japanese friend of mine got seriously ill and didn't tell me, as she didn't want to bother me with her problems! If I had been in her position, I would have announced it to the whole world, in order to win a bit of sympathy and moral support, but this sort of behaviour is strictly contrary to Japanese culture and mentality. Another Japanese friend of mine received a phone call from her best friend's husband, whilst we were having dinner in a Tokyo restaurant, to inform her that his wife was on her death bed (she had been suffering from terminal cancer) and ask her to come to the hospital. My friend burst out crying in the restaurant, to the shock and horror of all the other guests. After she had left, people started talking about how "stupid" it was of her to behave in the manner she had. She had disturbed the harmony and atmosphere of the evening.

The Japanese are also hard people to get to know. I have a friend whom I have "known" for the past thirty years and with whom I have communicated for many years, and yet I feel that I know little about her, or about the dozens of Japanese that I got to know during my stay in Japan. These people don't open up even when the initial ice has been broken and you feel you can really trust each other. It is mainly small talk that then occurs. But I'm the kind of person who will start to talk about everything and everyone to anyone I feel I can trust.

Family and Community

I GREW UP in a large family. Until shortly before my birth, my great-grandfather, his three sons (one being my grandfather) and their wives, his grandchildren (numbers varied from ten to nineteen, depending on who had been married off and who was visiting), his great-grandchildren (who were uncountable) and the numerous relatives visiting for longer periods of time all lived under one roof. Cooking was done on a daily basis for more than fifty people. When I was still small and my great-grandparents died, my grandfather and his brothers split up into three separate households, which nevertheless were next to each other and shared a common compound. There were between ten and fifteen members in our household. For sure, living in an extended family had its problems, but there were many advantages as well. We didn't lack for friends or have to make "appointments" to play with other children. There were plenty of kids in the compound for us to play with. My grandfather's brothers were like grandfathers to us. The second cousins were like first cousins. The numerous aunts and uncles had equal "status". There wasn't much differentiation. It was great in many ways to live in this extended family environment and I miss it tremendously. When I mention this to people in the West they are horrified. How could you have lived like that? What about privacy? Couples never went anywhere alone; there was usually a whole entourage following them.

I now live in a nuclear family composed of just the four of us, and my children often ask when their grandmother or some other relative will be leaving when they have come to visit or stay with us. We would have considered it very rude to ask someone how long they would be staying for. Even now I don't ask people directly how long they are coming for; I usually beat around the bush and figure out for myself when they are likely to leave. My children have their "best" or favored relatives and don't care much about the others. They have little respect for the extended family, and they are horrified when I insist upon them calling people of their parents' age or older Aunt or Uncle (they don't understand why non-relatives should be made into relatives out of respect). I know of many kids in Germany who call their parents by their first names because it is (apparently) a cool thing to do. My nieces and nephew on my husband's side call me by my name rather than "Auntie". Indians and Africans would be absolutely horrified by this. The surprising thing is that Germans are still quite strict about the use of the personal pronoun "Sie", the respectful form of the Second Person, for people (even of their own age) whom they have known for donkey's years.

Food and Eating Culture

FOOD PLAYS AN important role in Asian and African families and cultures. Eating together is a way of bonding, of sharing what God has given you, and also a way of spending quality time with people that you like. It wasn't unusual for us to have guests for lunch or dinner a couple of times a week at my parents' place. The quantity of food and the number of dishes will depend on what you can afford, but people try their best to fill up the table with as many dishes as possible in order not to look "stingy". Even the poor share whatever they might have with their guests, and don't feel shy about it or hide, or eat alone in front of others.

Despite having lived in the West for more than half my life now, I have still not come to terms with the phenomenon of people whom you know well getting out their food and starting to eat it in front of you without offering you anything. This still shocks me. The other cultures that I know would find this very rude. When I first started visiting German households, I often went home hungry or thirsty because no one (I believed) had offered me anything. It was always "help yourself", something I couldn't relate to. I find it strange eating other people's food without their having offered it to me. What if they really don't want you to have it? In Indian culture, people offer you food or drink a couple of times before you say "yes", and you don't normally say "yes" the first time. As this was what I was used to, I often went hungry or thirsty when I didn't accept the offer the first time round—because no German bothered to ask again! But I have learnt my lesson since.

Identity

As mentioned earlier, I am of Indian origin; I was born in Kenya; I studied in England; I have lived in many different countries in the last twenty years; I am married to a German; and I am a German citizen. So—what identity does this give me? Am I condemned to being a foreigner wherever I go?

Religion

When we were children, my siblings and numerous cousins and I visited the temple opposite our house in Kenya every evening. We sang the songs which were taught to us without giving much thought to the texts or their meaning. We prayed mainly for things like good grades. We ate the delicious offerings shared at the end of the prayers and then ran back home. For my primary schooling, I attended one of the Aga Khan schools, where we learnt about the Ismailis and prayed everyday for the well-being of His Highness the Aga Khan. My best friends were Sikhs and I learnt a bit about their religion from them. My secondary schooling was in a mainly Christian school, where we learnt a little about Christianity.

We didn't learn about the Hindu religion (the religion of my parents) as such, either at home or at school. We didn't really have a devotional "relationship" with any of the hundreds of Hindu gods. In fact, we feared God because we were taught—and this was indeed made clear to us—that if we did this or that (often things that happened to be against our parents' wishes), or we lied, God would punish us. If something stupid happened, it was therefore always an indication that God was punishing you. It is only recently that I have stopped fearing God and started loving Him, after realizing that He is not to be feared. I still don't know much about Hinduism, largely because of ignorance, but it does feel great not to have to fear God.

IN CONCLUSION: it has been difficult for me to condense and outline all the experiences I have had living in different countries and cultures. All I can say is that I have benefited tremendously from the experiences I have had, which have given me a kind of *multi-kulti* status. Having the feeling of being in transit all the time and not having a base to call home certainly does make life difficult, both emotionally and physically. But I have reached a point where I now know that I enjoy discovering other cultures and countries and that it will be difficult for me to settle down in any one place.

I have never really written about my experiences before, and writing this article has involved a great deal of self-discovery, leading me to wonderful memories and a deeper appreciation of all the cultures I have encountered over the years.

YOU, ME, AND "HUM"
BY MANJU RAMANAN

AUTHOR'S NOTE: *The title of this paper was inspired by the Hindi film* U, Me aur Hum *(dir. Ajay Devgan 2008), which means "you, me and us", but the inspiration ends there. The film is about love in the shadow of Alzheimer's, while this paper aims to show how "the Other"—"you", referring here to Indian tribals and denotified tribal communities—entered my life ("me"), blasting away deep-rooted prejudices and helping me gain a new perspective on the world (*hum, *or "us").*

I WAS BORN INTO an educated Tamil Brahmin family in Gujarat, and my introduction to "the Other" started with prejudices. I was around eight or ten years old, growing up in Baroda in the Eighties, when I noticed how some of the plumbers or masons from the Waghri community who came to our home to repair a toilet or fix a broken wall or tile would refuse to take the glass of water that I offered them. They would insist that I pour it from the glass into their cupped palm and then they would drink it. I was excited about the drama surrounding this event, but ignorant of the long tradition of prejudice of which it was part. My grandmother explained to me that since they were tribals (she would refer to them as Scheduled Castes) and worked among the toilets, *etc.*, they were presumably unclean and so they wouldn't want to leave any germs on the glass we offered. But didn't the germs affect *them*, too, since they drank the same water, and that with their bare hands? Some questions were left unanswered, and this was my sketchy initial introduction to the "Other". To the best of my childhood understanding and imagination, they were people who were unlike us: they lived far away in deep forests, a long way from technology and advancement, they ate differently, and their women smoked *beedis* (rolled tobacco leaves). I was also told that the tribal gods were not as benign-looking as ours. The story that fascinated me most as a child was one about the "Treemen of Travancore"—about tribals who lived in the trees. My father encountered it as a chapter in a school textbook in the Forties and recollected that it was written by a European traveler who had met and lived with this tribe—who lived up in the trees and feasted on tadpoles! (for the "treemen", see Iyer 1941).

Other prejudices were derived from Hindi cinema, which reinforced the idea that tribals (or *adivasis*) came mostly from the forest and usually wore grass skirts, clothes made of bark, or other revealing costumes. They sang and danced differently to the heroes and heroines of the films, and their songs were incomprehensible but catchy ("Hum Bewafa Hargiz na The" in *Shalimar*, 1978, released in the USA as *Raiders of Shalimar*, is a good example of such a song). Lee Fawk's *Phantom* comics, depicting white men ruling the tribal world of Africa, reinforced such ideas.

My prejudice would have carried on blissfully uninterrupted if things had not changed in college at Baroda. I was enjoying some inspirational English literature teaching at the Maharaja Sayajirao University, and learning about literary theory and the politicization of language, while doing postgraduate work. A highly respected professor, Dr. Ganesh Devy, a Sahitya Akademi winner and well-reputed scholar, quit his university job to start the Bhasha Research and Publication Center (BRPC), which set out to document tribal languages that were on the verge of extinction. The BRPC successfully launched a tribal magazine, *Dhol*, which documented tribal languages. In due course, it initiated a historical movement to address a pertinent part of tribal life—human rights. In 1998, the BRPC organised the Verrier Elwin lecture series in Baroda, commemorating the celebrated tribal activist Verrier Elwin (1902-64), a Christian missionary who had given up his vocation in order to work with Mahatma Gandhi, and found his calling with the Baiga and Gond tribes of central India. Elwin married a tribal woman, and served as Deputy Director of the Anthropological Survey of India upon its formation in 1945 (Guha 1999).

The first Verrier Elwin lecture was delivered by Magsaysay award winner and tribal activist Mahashveta Devi. She spoke about Budhan Sabar, a denotified tribal (DNT) killed in police custody. Budhan belonged to the Sabar tribe from Purulia district in West Bengal. He was traveling with his wife Shyamali Sabar to attend a wedding in a nearby village when the police inspector from Burabazar Police Station arrested him. The next day, his dead body was handed over to his wife—and the postmortem report stated that he had committed suicide in police custody. It was bizarre, since Budhan had no reasons for suicide and was about to attend a joyous occasion. The Sabars who worked closely with Mahashveta Devi told her about Budhan's death and, following her advice, did not cremate the body. To reassure the police that the body had been burned, however, the Sabars cleverly cremated an effigy, while Shyamali dug a hole in her hut, buried her husband's body in it, covered it with a mat and sat on it in mourning, until the moment when Mahashveta Devi arrived with a lawyer and another doctor. The second autopsy that was then conducted proved that his death had occurred *before* he was allegedly found hanging. Other evidence too pointed towards his death having been murder rather than suicide (Devi 1999).

Mahashveta Devi's speech moved me deeply. This, in combination with the emotions that I was experiencing in literature class, where there was a lot of heightened class-room discussion on literary theory connected with the politicization of language but hardly any follow-up in the form of action, compelled me to volunteer for the BRPC, which had now started the Denotified Tribals Rights Action Group to work for justice in the matter of

Budhan's custodial death.

For my postgraduate degree I had chosen to study institutional racism—a term coined by Stokely Carmichael of the Black Panther Party, who, in the late Sixties, defined it as "the collective failure of an organization to provide an appropriate and professional service to people because of their color, culture, or ethnic origin"—and what it had done to three minority communities of Canada: the First Nations, the Japanese- and the Chinese-Canadians. In class I was learning how prejudiced and subversive laws and regulations formulated by imperialism influenced and shaped the writings of the above-mentioned minorities in Canada. Imperial rule had annihilated so many tribes there by either hunting them like animals, gifting them diseased blankets and wiping them all out, or "befriending them" for trade. In the book *Shananditti: The Last of the Beothuks*, the last living member of the Beothuk tribe from Newfoundland tells her story (Winter 1975). At the BRPC, I had the chance to meet DNTs, some of whom had been born in police custody, had endured third-degree torture in jails, or were victims of false accusation due to an outdated and prejudiced system.

According to Devy (1998), the estimated population of the DNTs is around sixty million, and in India there are about 191 communities that were once wrongly "notified" as "criminal tribes", owing to the colonial government's lack of understanding of the nomadic way of life. They were restricted by law to specific localities, prevented from moving, put to unpaid labour and stigmatized beyond redemption. After their "de-notification" in 1952, these communities, now known as DNTs, continued to suffer stigma, social isolation and acute economic disadvantage. Utterly dispossessed, these landless, illiterate and hounded people have been unsuccessfully trying to shake off their identity.

It was appalling to learn how prejudice became a potent weapon of domination and discrimination. According to the historian and tribal activist Ajay Dandekar, in his essay "The Hegemony of Silence":

In the nineteenth century the colonial government decided to categorize these pastoral nomads, itinerant traders and other disbanded groups who include the members of defeated native armies and other wandering communities as different from those settled agriculturists of a fixed abode. The then administration decided that these wandering communities could not be situated within preconceived categorisations—whether administrative, economic or social. This was the context to the passage of the "Criminal Tribes Act of 1871" or Act XXVII - (henceforth referred to as the CTA) (16).

Dandekar explains how it is important to look at the legal provisions of the CTA. The act stated:

> Whereas it is expedient to provide for the registration, surveillance and control of certain criminal tribes and eunuchs, it is thereby enacted as follows: This Act may be called "The Criminal Tribes Act, 1871". [Commencement, repealed by Act XVI of 1874, section 1 and Schedule, Part I.] This section and section 20 extend to the whole of British India […] to be in force in the whole or any part of the territories under its government (17).

The CTA gave unrestricted access to the imperial government to prey on the communities listed under it. As Devy (1998) says:

> Many of the wandering minstrels, fakirs, petty traders, rustic transporters and disbanded groups of soldiers were included by the British in their list of criminal groups. During the first half of the nineteenth century, the tribes in the North West frontier had been declared "criminal tribes". This category became increasingly open ended and by 1871 the British had

prepared an official list of Criminal Tribes. An act to regulate criminal tribes was passed that year. For instance, Bhils who had fought the British rule in Kandesh and on the banks of Narmada and were convicted under section 110 of the IPC were to be recognised as criminal tribes.

This act was modified in 1952, five years after Indian independence, but it was merely a name-change. The "Criminal Tribes" were re-christened "Denotified Tribes"—the criminality being removed solely from the nomenclature—though in reality attitudes towards the DNTS and discrimination meted out to them stayed the same. What is more, this was followed by the introduction of a series of acts generally known as Habitual Offenders Acts!

The HOAs preserved most of the provisions of the former CT Acts, except the premise implicit in it that an entire community can be "born" criminal. Apparently, the denotification and the passing of the HOAs should have ended the misery of the communities penalized under the CT Act. But that has not happened. The police force as well as the people in general were taught to look upon the "Criminal Tribes" as born criminals during the colonial times. That attitude continues to persist even today (Devy 1998).

Sidelined by mainstream society, without too many opportunities owing to the prejudice associated with their names, castes, caste certificates and surnames, many DNTs are naturally pulled into the world of petty crime—ironically reinforcing the very prejudice against them. On my first day at the BRPC, I met a Gond tribal man from the city who had come to meet Dr. Devy. I was horrified to see that he had a dagger stuck to his left wrist, which was bleeding profusely. To arrest the blood flow, he had used a dirty kerchief. It was a perfect anti climax when, having read my thoughts, he let me into his secret: "Ben, yeh to spring hai" ("Sister, this is a spring"), showing me how the dagger was a roughly-made gadget, the blood animal blood, and the whole thing merely a ploy to garner sympathy and collect money from passers-by. This, I learned later, was one of the professions chosen by DNTs, involving a macabre kind of entertainment from the show of self-mutilation.

A case that happened at about the same time was that of a tribal from the Bajania community who had been killed by the upper caste Patels for stealing a bottle gourd from their orchard. Ironically, he belonged to a group of worshipers of the Bahucharaji goddess—a group that refrains from eating gourd as part of their religious rules. The dying man had named his killers, but power and bribes had prevented justice from being done. Another case was that of Pinya Hari Kale, who was arrested and then killed in police custody, though his death was investigated and compensation awarded (D'Souza 1999).

The DNT RAG campaign took up issues like these and received an overwhelming response from the de-notified communities—soon a journal called *Budhan* was started, the Budhan Sabar case was reopened and it was proved that he was killed in police custody and did not commit suicide. His wife Shyamali Sabar was awarded compensation, something never before heard of.

As Susan Abraham in her article *Steal or I'll Call You a Thief* (1999) has written:

> In a public interest litigation filed by Mahashweta Devi before the Calcutta High Court after the death of Budhan Sabar in police custody, Justice Ruma Pal passed a historical judgment on August 6th, 1998, ordering a CBI enquiry into Budhan Sabar's death, the immediate transfer of inspector Ashoke Roy and Rs 1 lakh [100,000 rupees, approx. 2,200 US dollars in 2010—*Ed.*] compensation to Budhan Sabar's widow. In the case of Pinya Hari Kale a writ petition has been

filed by Laxman Gaikwad in the Bombay High Court (1753).

This stirred up a hornet's nest and cases of atrocities against DNTs and custodial deaths started pouring in from different states of India. We received photographs, documents, complainants and cases on a regular basis, many of which became stories for the journal *Budhan*. The stand that DNT RAG took was challenging—through networking with academics, activists, writers and tribal leaders and the media across India, it had to create awareness of the issue—an issue that involved half a million people and deep-rooted prejudices, left over from the colonial era, that DNTS are genetically criminal.

The colonial administration in the nineteenth century, helped propagate this idea of criminality by coming up with a list of criminal tribes across India, sometimes cordoning off areas they lived in, making it mandatory for them to report to the nearby police station everyday and, most brutal of all, introducing the CT list into the curriculum for police schools across India (D'Souza), so that both British as well as Indian students would learn to hate and condemn the CTs. On the other hand, there was the challenge of not over-romanticizing the DNT population—after all, some of them *did* indulge in petty crime and thievery (see Dutt 2003). DNT RAG worked towards winning justice for vulnerable DNTs who were victims of a flawed system. As Devy (2008) says:

> We had exposed a long-festering wound. As a leader of that campaign I had to give very serious thought to turning the anger and frustration among the demonized, brutalized and politically vandalized DNT into a constructive energy. I decided to use the most ancient method of getting people angry without making them destructive—theater. My experience with handling the violence within the minds of these communities has left me convinced that theater is probably the most

powerful cultural means of sensitizing communities on the mutual entanglement and dependence of economic, social and cultural rights of several competing and clashing social sectors.

Using theater as a means of working with the DNTS can be well illustrated with DNT RAG's work with the Chharas, an educated community of DNTs from the Kubernagar area near Ahmedabad in Gujarat. The Chharas are known to brew liquor illegally with help from none other than the state police—ironically, in a state where alcohol is prohibited! Police personnel pay an inter-departmental bribe to be stationed at Chharanagar so as then to be able to extort money from the Chharas for indulging in a state-prohibited activity (Ramanan 2006).

DNT RAG started work with the Chharas by setting up a library on their premises, and getting together a group of Chharas to form their own theatre group, aptly named the Budhan theater group. Headed by Daxin Chhara, the group stages plays based on true incidents of atrocities against denotifed Indian tribals who are treated as born criminals by the legal system and as thieves by mainstream society, including plays about the treatment of Budhan Sabar of Purulia, West Bengal, Deepak Pawar of Maharashtra, and so on. The plays reflect the inhuman treatment meted out to DNTs and appeal to people to respect them and take their human dignity into account. As Daxin told me:

> Budhan Theatre is a volunteer theater group of [the] Chhara tribe. [The] Chhara tribe is one of the denotified tribes, [...] branded by law as "born criminals" by [the] British. Presently, based in Ahmedabad, this community is a "forever suspect" in the eye[s] of law and order and mainstream society and treated as a "hardcore criminal". Police atrocity and harassment is a regular practice among the Chhara tribe as well as among other denotified tribes of India. Budhan Theater is trying to remove the criminal stigma attached

to the Chhara tribe through theater, which we believe is our inherited talent. Through theater we are sensitising society towards social acceptance and legal justice. The DNTs have lost their identity due to living on the fringes of society. So many years after Independence, these communities and their people [still] have no constitutional guarantees. Budhan Theater is a cultural platform to protest and to raise the voice of the denotified and nomadic communities and fight for social justice and human dignity (E-mail from Daxin Chhara; see also *Budhan Theatre*, website).

The Bhasha Trust established the Adivasi Academy at Tejgadh in 1999. Since 2000, it has been teaching young men and women Tribal Studies—the study and understanding of how *adivasis* perceive the world. The idea is to make students reflect on their own situation, to motivate them and help them start about the great task of empowering *adivasi* villages by helping them to become self-reliant. The academy offers short-term training in microfinance, and diploma courses in tribal rights, food security and development, publication and rural journalism, and tribal arts and museum studies.

The varied activities of the BRPC shaped my perspective on the world. In December 1998, DNT RAG organized the All India DNT Convention, at which various DNTS from all over India along with theorists like Gayatri Chakraborty Spivak and historians like Romila Thapar participated in a common forum. Probably for the first time in their lives many DNTs realized that people like themselves existed all over India—and shared a common heritage of prejudice. All of us watched wide-eyed as we discovered the wealth that Indian tribal communities possessed—the history and culture that they had inherited—as well as the subversive laws that they were battling, years after India won her independence. This included, for example, a tribe from Maharashtra who were adept at sign language—and who demonstrated their unique skill. A man standing at one end of a room with a big *dhol* (drum) asked me my name and, after I had whispered it to him, beat a tune accompanied by some hand movements and his tribesman standing at the other end of the room shouted it out. It is said that the tribe used their unique ability as a means of passing on information about enemy attacks during the rule of the famous Maratha king Chhatrapati Shivaji.

One of the most remarkable tribal men that I met was the former pickpocket, now turned award winning writer, Laxman Gaikwad, from the Pardhi tribe. During an interview (I had become a journalist with *The Times of India* in Baroda), he explained how things had changed for him after he "abandoned the blade and took to the pen". His 1987 autobiography *Uchalya* (*The Branded*) was honored by India's National Academy of Letters in 1988.

> The razor blade was our Laxmi [Lakshmi, goddess of fortune and beauty, and the granter of wealth—*Ed.*]. We would pray to the god of instruments (Ayudha) before every outing. We would cut a chicken with the same blade and spray its blood on the participants, and we prayed: "God, we pray for success in today's thieving mission. Rescue us from the police if we get caught..." (based on Vikas Kamat's translation of excerpts from the original Marathi, online).

As for fear of the police, who usually hunted them down, he says:

> We were very afraid of the police. I cannot count the times I have defecated in my clothes during police tortures. My community members started hating my grandfather, as he was giving inside information to the police. "Because of Lingappa [his grandfather—*Ed.*] life has become hard; we are not able to feed our wives and children," they complained. One day, they held a

meeting to decide the next course of action. That night, they stuffed grandpa's mouth with rags, and killed him with an axe. They even burnt his body to destroy any evidence. That is how grandmother became head of the family (based on Kamat's translation).

This subaltern world existed parallel to my own—had been shielded from me, presumably by my protected upbringing, a life that had the time and the luxury to ponder over and romanticize suffering, though without feeling even a pinch of the harsh reality. But for "them", it was the only way of life that they knew. This was brought home to me when I interviewed several members of the DNT community, including Sushma Andhare from the Kolhati community. Sushma had resisted family pressure, and endured neglect and isolation, because she wanted to study, rather than joining the family profession of being a tamasha dancer, where young girls are taught the traditional tamasha dance and soon exposed to the ugly world of prostitution. Mentored by the DNT activist Laxman Mane, Sushma opted to study and do a doctorate instead, and now has several books to her credit.

Colonial attitudes towards aboriginal peoples are common throughout the world—long after the end of colonialism—and upper caste attitudes towards the *adivasis* of India are an example of this. While one can blame imperialism and the various tools it used to contain what it believed to be criminal, the casteist mindset hasn't allowed this prejudice to be exorcised in the way that it should be.

Movements like the DNT RAG have now moved online, through *Mukt-Saad*, a web publication from Baroda maintained by India's National Folklore Support Center, which is contributing to the gradual sensitization in India to the issue of DNTs.

THE DNTs ARE part of my life—they have shaped the course my life has taken. They are instrumental in helping me in my quest to blur the difference between "you", "me" and *hum*.

References

Abraham, Susan. "Steal or I'll Call You a Thief: 'Criminal' Tribes of India." In: *Economic and Political Weekly*, July 3rd, 1999, 1751-53.

Budhan Theatre: The Official Budhan Theatre Website, <http://budhantheatre.org/blog/page/2/>

Chhara, Daxin / Gagdekar, Roxy. Email to the author, December 27th, 2008.

Dandekar, Ajay. "A Hegemony of Silence: The Case of India's Denotified Tribes." In: *Counter-Hegemony and the Postcolonial "Other"*. Ed. Michael Hayes / Thomas Acton. Newcastle-upon-Tyne: Cambridge Scholars Press, 2006, 14-27.

Devi, Mahasveta Devi. "Born 1871—India's Denotified Tribes." In: *Budhan*, February-March, 1999. Baroda: Bhasha Research and Publication Center, 1999, 9-13.

Devy, Ganesh. "The Branded Tribes of India." In: *PUCL Bulletin*, 9, 1998. Delhi: People's Union for Civil Liberties.

------------. "Giving Adivasis a Voice." In: *InfoChange India News & Features*, October 2008. Website, <http://infochangeindia.org/Agenda/Against-exclusion/Giving-adivasis-a-voice.html>

D'Souza, Dilip. "De-Notified Tribes: Still Criminal?" In: *Economic and Political Weekly*, December 18th-24th, 1999, 3576-78.

Dutt, Nabanita. "Paradhis of India: A Tribe of Hereditary Criminals." In: *Trickster's Way*, 2, 3, July 15th, 2003. Website, <http://digitalcommons.trinity.edu/cgi/viewcontent.cgi?article=1065&context=tricksersway>

[Gaekwad, Laxman.] "Uchalya: The Caste of the Criminals". Excerpts from Gaekwad's novel (1988) transl. by Vikas Kamat. In: *kamat's potpourri*, Website, <http://www.kamat.com/econtent/reviews/books/uchalya.htm> N. B. A full translation (*The Branded*), by P. A. Kolharkar, was published by Sahitya Akademi (New Delhi) in 1999.

Guha, Ramchandra. *Savaging the Civilized: Verrier Elwin,*

His Tribals, and India. Chicago: University of Chicago Press; 1999.

Iyer, L. A. Krishna. *The Aborigines of Travancore (The Travancore Tribes and Castes, 3)*. Trivandrum: Government Press, 1941.

Mukt-Saad (Call of the Unbound). An interdisciplinary bilingual journal focused on the Nomadic and the Denotified Communities of India. Website, <http://www.indianfolklore.org/journals/index.php/mukt>

Ramanan, Manju. "We Are Not Thieves." In: *Femina Special Issue*, December 20th, 2006, 172-82.

Winter, Keith John. *Shananditti: The Last of the Beothuks*. North Vancouver: J. J. Douglas, 1975.

THE POOPING QUEEN: REFLECTIONS ON THE OWN AND THE OTHER

BY PAUL HARRISON

FOR AS LONG as I can remember, I have been fascinated by religious, cultural and linguistic contrasts. The experiences of my early childhood brought me into contact with people of a variety of different origins and persuasions, encouraging me to take a comparative view of things. I was aware from an early age that various religions, cultures and languages have certain basic traits in common, whereas the specific forms which our religious, cultural and linguistic practices take depend on accidents of birth.

The accident of my birth deposited me in Felton Crescent, a little cul-de-sac adjacent to Saltwell Park in Gateshead, over the river from Newcastle-upon-Tyne in the north-east of England. Our semi-detached house and the others in the "Crescent" (as we called it) were built on the site where Ferndene House had once stood, a sprawling Gothic mansion first owned by Robert Stirling Newall, a wizard-like man with a long white beard who was Mayor of Gateshead for two years. Newall's company manufactured the cable used to tow Cleopatra's Needle up the Thames in London, the first cross-channel cable and half of the first transatlantic one. He was also the owner of the then largest refractor telescope in the world, which the King of Belgium apparently came to see on one occasion.

I have in my possession a yellowing old photograph showing Newall sitting on a contraption mounted on circular rails inside his observatory in the grounds of Ferndene House, peering through one of the eyepieces of the huge telescope. The telescope was later moved to Cambridge and finally to the observatory on Mount Penteli near Athens in Greece. After further research I discovered that later inhabitants of Ferndene House included a Mr. T. Bogue, a *Class B Certified Controlled and Inspirational Speaker* at Spiritualist churches and a subscribing member of the Spiritualists' National Union. Bogue took part in Spiritualist séances, something my grandmother seems to have dabbled in too, if the remarks of my mother on the subject are anything to go by. Ferndene House later became a Roman Catholic convent school.

This was all unknown to me and my family at the time, of course, but perhaps the echoes of so much research into the "Other"—astronomical, esoterical or otherwise—on the site of the front bedroom in which I was later born seeped into me somehow, kindling an interest in taking the Other and making it my own, a habit which was to become a constant thread running through my life. The deterioration of my short-term memory being more than made up for by the memories of long ago which are now surfacing on a daily basis, this seems as good a time as any to reflect upon the influences which helped to form this habit of mine, the areas it affected and the repercussions it has had for my perception—and understanding—of what I started out with all those years ago.

Some of my earliest recollections are of foreign coins popping up in various drawers and down the sides of armchairs. They were often accompanied by postage stamps with strange foreign inscriptions or by photographs of my father, sunburnt and wearing white shorts, in the presence of other similarly-clad men on a ship off the coast of Curaçao or wherever it was. My father worked for Shell as first officer in the Merchant Navy in those days, and that explains how all those tokens of far-away places found their way into our house.

My mother was a nurse, so she had friends, colleagues and patients of a variety of origins and religious persuasions, including Protestants, Catholics, Hindus, Sikhs and Jews. The latter were particularly numerous, Gateshead also being known as "Little Jerusalem" due to the large numbers of Jews who had settled there at various times, founding a sizeable Jewish neighborhood in the process. There was a Talmud school and a German-Jewish bakery sporting a sign reading "Stenhouse" on one side and "Steinhaus" on the other, and little boys with ringlets accompanied bearded men in black hats sitting on the benches facing the park lake. There were several Jewish families living in the Crescent then, and, like my sister, I soon became a "shabbat goy" who did all the things Jews aren't allowed to do on the Sabbath, such as switching lights on and off and adjusting the time switch on the deep-freeze. I remember that the houses smelled differently than ours did, and after doing my job I was rewarded with an exotic-tasting home-made biscuit or was allowed to hang a star up in the tabernacle, the portable worship facility erected for the Feast of the Tabernacles, Israel's Thanksgiving feast.

And then there was Sunday lunch at Pindi's (full name Beppindo Singh), a Sikh doctor colleague of my mother's, at his home in a now long-demolished area of Newcastle. I can recall spicy food and sweet sugary desserts and the lady of the house not being able to pronounce the word "crisp", saying "crips" instead. I also remember meeting the Singhs at the tea counter at Shephard's of Gateshead, our local department store, and asking them how to pronounce "Darjeeling", a name I had seen on a tea-chest. Perhaps experiences such as these were some of the first signs of my later interest in languages.

The first school attended by my sister and me was a private one called Musgrave, which was housed in another Gothic mansion and run by two bewhiskered old ladies, Miss Elliot and Miss Evelyn. The Jewish girls at Musgrave School trooped into the hall after the Christian part of the morning assembly, which included a sermon and hymn-singing. Boys were in the minority at Musgrave. They usually left at age eight, going on to the Royal Grammar School, after which Musgrave was for girls only.

Unfortunately, I failed the entrance examination to the "RGS", as we called it, so I was sent to the rough-and-tumble local council school instead. It was quite a culture shock for me to experience for the first time the various seasonal games and rituals involving "conkers" and "liggees", which were the words for chestnuts and marbles in Geordie, the dialect spoken in the area. My father was a Londoner and my mother didn't speak broad Geordie, so I spoke a very moderate version of the dialect, if at all. This made me a minority of one among the pupils at Kelvin Grove School, who spoke in a way which my teachers at Musgrave had taught me to avoid as it was "common".

At Musgrave, I was made to feel guilty if I spoke like the kids around me, and now those kids made my life a misery because I didn't talk like them. I recall one boy at Kelvin Grove School saying "Thinks yersel' posh!" ("You think you're posh!"), and another one saying "Aah hate that lad!" ("I hate that boy!") to his schoolmates. One of the girls wondered why my parents had sent me to a private school: "Did they think you were too expensive to go to a normal one?" she asked. When I confronted my father about this, he said, "Tell them it was to give a good grounding to your education." It didn't give much of a grounding to my new social life, I'm afraid.

At one point I tried talking like a local to see how my parents would react: "Oh, yer hev—aah knaa yer hev" ("Oh, you have—I know you have") I said in answer to some question as we were getting into the car one day, and I was promptly scolded for it by my horrified mother. The fact that my father was from London and said things like "Go up the apples and pears to Uncle Ned" (Cockney rhyming slang for "Go upstairs to bed") was, I suppose, also a contributing factor in my having rather different cultural and linguistic horizons than most of my schoolmates.

My parents being from different social spheres, one of

the typical features of my childhood was the juxtaposition of contrasts. A typical instance of this was going to a Christmas party at the upper-crust "International Marine Association" one day and then attending the altogether more modest affair held at "Whitehall Road Methodist Church" the next. For most of the children I went to school with, however, life was strictly compartmentalized. On the other side of the road to Kelvin Grove School was a Roman Catholic one—a different world entirely for most of my schoolmates, who called Catholics "Cathies" and told tales of draconian Monday-morning punishments for children who had not been to church on Sunday. The Jews fared no better among my fellow pupils—they called them "sheenies", and gave them a three-finger salute which apparently meant "You killed Christ".

By contrast, Jews and Catholics were physically very close in the Crescent, a thin wall being all that separated my mother's Catholic friend Catherine from the Books next door, a Jewish family from Germany. Not that I hadn't noticed the differences between "us" and "them", of course. My mother ordered *Knowledge* magazine for me at the newsagent's, the monthly instalments of which we collected and bound in the glossy blue binder one could buy for the purpose. *Knowledge* told me about gravity on the moon, the journeys of Marco Polo, and all kinds of things which were beyond the horizons of my schoolmates. I first became aware of the existence of competing world-views when I showed Julia, the elder daughter of the Books, an artist's impression of the young Earth as a ball of burning gases and she said "I don't believe that".

Maybe the ghostly presence of Newall's telescope lived on in my enthusiasm for astronomy and science fiction. When I was still quite small, my mother showed me how to identify the constellations of the Plough and Orion in the sky at night, *The Sky at Night* also being the name of a television program featuring eccentric astronomer Patrick Moore that I loved to watch. Every now and then my mother would send me off in the dark to borrow something from her friend Catherine a few doors down, and I can still recall the strange delight I experienced as I stood in our quiet cul-de-sac for a few moments, feeling the nip in the air and smelling the coal fires we had in those days. I can remember looking up at the stars and shivering with a mixture of fear and pleasure before hurrying off on my errand.

A paperback collection of science fiction stories which I begged my mother to buy for me at our local department store soon widened my horizons to inner and outer space, and I found myself absolutely spellbound by a television series about a reluctant time traveler called *Dr. Who*. I can still recall my puzzled mother telling a neighbor that she didn't quite know what to say when I tried to explain the fourth dimension to her (something I had learned about from *Dr. Who*). I became even more besotted with space when I visited the planetarium in Baker Street in London—and when I went to see the film *2001: A Space Odyssey* by Stanley Kubrick. This gave me a cosmic view of things, elements of which I had already gleaned from H. G. Wells's *History of the World* and other fictional and non-fictional writings of his on the future of mankind.

And, who knows, perhaps the spirit presence of Inspirational Speaker Mr. T. Bogue of Ferndene House had its echoes in the religious eclecticism of my upbringing. Spiritualists are not committed to any one single religion, instead drawing their inspiration and their methods of worship from a number of different religious and philosophical traditions. My experiences with various religions as a child led me in a similar direction, and I can remember doing my best to explain my views in a talk on reincarnation which I was scheduled to hold in my English class at secondary school. As it happened, I was unable to hold my talk due to illness and the teacher read it out in my absence, so I don't know how my classmates reacted to it. I subsequently strayed from the fold of the austere Methodist church which I had attended since I was very small, trying out various other churches instead. I remember being especially taken by the High Anglican church with its sense of ceremony and its candle-lit processions.

There was the American connection too. I often used to go to the corner shop near to where my grandmother lived and buy *Marvel* and *DC* comics about Batman, Superman and the Incredible Hulk. The world these superheroes inhabited contrasted sharply with the run-down surroundings of the shop, an area long since demolished in the name of slum clearance. There were some Americans among my parents' friends: Captain Williams, for instance, who gave me a T-shirt with eyes that moved, and Al Foster, who delighted me with the gift of a dollar note bearing his autograph. My schoolmates didn't believe it was genuine, however—"It's Confederate!" they exclaimed, referring to the fake Confederate States dollar notes being given away with bubble gum or some such commodity at the time. As it happened, an American I met years later told me that my United States dollar wasn't actually legal tender, as it had been defaced by the autograph.

Television in those days was dominated by American productions like *The Dick Van Dyke Show*, *The Mary Tyler Moore Show*, *The Lucy Show*, *The Addams Family*, *The Munsters*, *The Banana Splits*, *The Monkees*, Hanna-Barbera cartoons, and *Fireball* and *Thunderbirds* by Gerry and Silvia Anderson. To me, America was a mixture of the Own and the Other, a parallel universe in which everything, language included, was strangely familiar and yet alien at the same time. And how glamorous New York sounded when talked about in an American accent on the top deck of a bus trundling through the Gateshead slums!

The first *border* I ever encountered was little more than a sign reading "Scotland" on one side and "England" on the other, a popular place to pose for photographs on the Great North Road from London to Edinburgh. I still possess a series of snaps of my father, my mother, my sister and myself arranged in various combinations around the sign. My paternal grandmother lived in a small fishing village called Eyemouth, just over the border, and we often went there for our summer holidays. I can vividly remember waking up in a room smelling of mothballs and going out blinking into the brilliant sunshine with my sister. First thing each morning we'd walk down to the end of the road past the two ladies who sat outside their houses at the corner saying, "Are you going to see the sea?" with a charming Scottish lilt in their voice.

The language used there was still English, of course, whereas later on in life I mainly encountered the Other by learning languages other than my own. My first conscious brush with foreign tongues was when I discovered a large red-backed multilingual dictionary owned by Catherine, my mother's Catholic friend. It was for English, German, French and Yiddish, and I remember being struck by the fact that Yiddish looked rather similar to German.

The early interest in French which this book brought about was quashed somewhat by the unsuccessful attempts of my French teacher at secondary school to teach us French audio-visually, using slides of little cartoon characters populating a cartoon Paris and saying things like *Ici l'église de la Madeleine*. In spite of this trendy addition, the methods were still quite old-fashioned in those days: we had a French vocabulary test every day, and each word we didn't get right had to be written out a hundred times at home. This was more like a punishment than an encouragement to go on a voyage of linguistic discovery, which is what learning a new language should really be.

It wasn't until we moved to Germany in 1970 that learning other languages began in earnest for me. As an adolescent whose voice had only just recently broken, it was vitally important for me to be able to integrate with my peers. The result was a high motivation to learn German which prompted me to stay up until the early hours of the morning practicing German grammar.

Emden, where we lived for the first three years, was the site of some early practical lessons in cultural relativism. At school in England, I had been told to keep my hands *under* the desk, whereas in Germany schoolchildren were required to keep their hands *on top* of it. For everyone else, keeping my hands under the desk meant I had bad manners, so for social reasons I soon adapted. For me, however, the reactions to my behavior demonstrated something I had already noticed with regard to religion: a society needs rules adhered to by all, but the precise forms which these rules take differ, depending on where you happen to have been born and raised. It struck me then that it was just the same with language: all human beings have the need to communicate, but the language they use to do so is determined by circumstances beyond their control.

I noticed the different national angles on things (and the fundamental similarities between them) when my sister married a German. An uncle of mine whose cousin had been killed by a German in the war said: "The only good German is a dead German." It turned out that my sister's father-in-law had a relative who had been killed by an Englishman in the war, so he in turn believed that "The only good Englishman is a dead Englishman". A rather poignant variation on this theme occurred when my mother worked in an old people's home years later and was dressing an old man's war wound when he said: "It's strange—an English person gave it to me and an English person is putting it right again."

My family spent a lot of their time in the company of the British, Americans, Canadians, Norwegians and Belgians who made up the international community in Emden and worked at the Rheinstahl Nordseewerke shipyard building container ships. The customers being Indian, there was a swastika on the bow of the first ship to be launched—an object of horror to the German nationals attending the ceremony. Of course, thanks to the intercultural competence which my early experiences had instilled in me, I was well aware of the ancient Indian origins of this potent symbol.

At that time we lived in a small village, three kilometers to the west of Emden, in which Low German was spoken. I decided not to learn this language, sensing that High German would be more useful to me when I moved elsewhere. Instead of *zwanzig Pfennig*, as in High German, in Larrelt (as the village was called) they said something closer to *twintig penning*, which is just a breath away from the English equivalent "twenty pennies".

Emden was not far from the border to the Netherlands, and we went shopping there once or twice because the shops sold things we knew from England, like baked beans and peanut butter. There was a telephone box on each side of the border. The one on the German side said *Telefon* with a capital "T" and one "o", while the one on the Dutch side said *telefoon* with a small "t" and two "o"s. This intrigued me. When we crossed the "border" into Scotland, the accent changed, but the language was basically the same, and here was a place where you only had to walk a few meters and the language was different. Not entirely, however—as the above example shows, there were great similarities between German and Dutch, and they could be put to use for learning Dutch with the help of German as a "contrast language", which I subsequently did.

After three years we moved to Hamburg, where my teachers gave me a rather better grounding in French than my teachers in England had. I then graduated from High School and studied philosophy for seven years, the only visible result of which was an intermediate thesis on "The pre-philosophical origins of Greek philosophical thought". After visiting Amsterdam in the Netherlands several times, I finally moved there, living on various houseboats. It struck me how differently I was treated depending on whether I spoke English or German, there still being quite a lot of anti-German sentiment about in the Netherlands in those days.

Back in Germany, I moved to Hildesheim near Hanover in 1984, where I studied for a degree in technical translation. I was able to perfect my French there with the help of an excellent teacher who was a native speaker of the language. Spanish, on the other hand, I learned on my own, though using a book written by another of the lecturers, also a native speaker. It was then that I realized the benefits of teaching yourself one language in contrast to another one closely related to it that you already know, learning large parts of the new vocabulary by discovering the typical transpositions required as you move from one language to the other.

My knowledge of Spanish improved as a result of my trips to Lanzarote and El Hierro in the Canary Islands and to the Dominican Republic in the Caribbean. The forms of Spanish which I encountered there had certain traits in common, the most obvious being the pronunciation of "c" before a high vowel as a sharp "s" instead of the lisping "th" sound that I knew from the Spanish of a large part of the Iberian Peninsula. Another place sharing this pronunciation was Vigo in Galicia in northwest Spain, where I went to teach English on a short exchange visit subsidized by the ERASMUS program of the European Union.

Vigo not being far from the Portuguese border, I took a bus trip to Porto in northern Portugal one weekend, and I immediately fell in love with the city. During the journey I had a similarly striking contrastive experience to the one I had had on the Dutch border years before: when the bus crossed the border into Portugal, the radio station we were listening to suddenly switched from a Spanish to a Portuguese one, and I was immediately struck by the contrast between the abruptness of Spanish and the softer sounds and stresses of Portuguese. This was also obvious when I returned to Vigo on the Sunday evening: when the train crossed the border into Spain, the gentle sibilants of the Portuguese passengers were increasingly drowned out by the staccato sounds of the Spanish passengers boarding the train.

By then I had largely made Spanish my own, and for me it became the slightly dull contrast language which I used as a background for teaching myself Portuguese, just as French had been the contrast language when I learned Spanish, and German had when I learned Dutch. I knew the typical systematic differences in pronunciation and vocabulary and was soon able to change a Spanish utterance into one that sounded fairly Portuguese, although I had to bear in mind that Portuguese sometimes uses totally different words than Spanish does for the same phenomenon, for example *janela* in place of *ventana* for English "window".

On my first visit to Porto, I went to a concert by the well-known Portuguese singer Carlos de Carmo. It was a moving experience to hear the whole auditorium sing along to a song likening Lisbon to a young girl: *Lisboa menina y moça*. I read all about the history of Portugal and felt even closer to the country on my next visit there, which was on the 25th anniversary of the end of the dictatorship in 1974. The signal for the so-called "carnation revolution" to begin had been the playing of a Portuguese folk song, *Grandola Vila Morena*, and on the 25th anniversary of this bloodless uprising people walked the streets of Porto singing it. Having been taught the words by a young lady on the bus from Vigo during my previous visit, I was able to sing along with them. This experience made me feel I was getting under the skin of the country and its people—a thing I believe you can do with music and song better than with anything else.

The next language to interest me was Turkish, mainly because a friend and I planned to go there on holiday. My friend booked the flights and agreed to drive us around the country in a hired car, while I learned the language and drew up the itinerary. To me it was a strange country with alien customs at first, but again, knowing at least the rudiments of the language soon made me feel more at home there. The tapes I used to learn Turkish included a situation in the café on the platform of Sirkeci station on the Bosporus in Istanbul in which a lady ordered a Pepsi: *Bana bir Pepsi lütfen* ("I'll have a Pepsi, please"). The first linguistic task I had set myself for Istanbul was to go to that very same café and say *Bana bir Pepsi lütfen*, just like in my Turkish course, and I did so soon after arriving.

To learn Turkish, I couldn't resort to any of the languages I already knew, but my knowledge of other cultures came in handy here too. For example, "holiday" in Turkish is *tatil*, and I remembered it by thinking of the film *Mr. Hulot's Holiday* by French director Jacques Tati. The surname "Tati" plus the "l" in the middle of "holiday" gave me "tatil". Music did its work in Turkey too, and I soon felt quite at home with the exotic rhythms and harmonies of the songs. I subsequently developed a fascination for mosques, and whenever we passed a mosque I couldn't wait to get my shoes off and feel the softness of the carpets beneath my stockinged feet. I remember finding the faint odor of feet which pervades these places of worship not at all unpleasant.

So accustomed was I to the sights, sounds and smells of the country that I didn't want to leave again. On the bus taking us out to the plane at Ankara Airport, I saw a Turkish family who were taking Grandma out to America to live there for the rest of her life. I felt touched to hear her wailing and praying to Allah: "Oh protect me Allah, I am a poor old woman and I am leaving the land of my fathers, never to return." It took a while for a kind man to calm her down, and it took me a while to calm down too—I didn't want to go either, feeling totally at home with the language, the culture and the rugged landscape.

By now my method of learning languages included finding a native speaker of the language in question and practicing the pronunciation with them. For example, the departmental secretary of the Institute of Applied Linguistics at Hildesheim University became my informant for Turkish pronunciation. The classes in oral English competence which I taught at the university were attended by exchange students from various countries, so this was a good opportunity for me to make a deal with some of them: "You learn my language and I'll learn yours," I told them. Some Polish girls attended my courses one year, and this was my big chance to get started with the Slavic languages.

For me, learning a language is usually part of the preparations for visiting the country in which it is spoken, and Polish was no exception. Some friends of mine had planned a trip to Masuria, a region of lakes and forests which used to be part of Germany ("East Prussia") and now belongs to Poland. One of the ladies I went with was going there in search of her roots, having been born on a farm in a small village in Masuria. There was nothing left of the farm now—all we could see when we got there were endless fields of corn, the legacy of long years of collectivist agriculture.

What struck me as especially fascinating on my first trip to Poland was that, having been resettled with Poles after the Germans fled westwards from the onslaught of the Russian army, the same landscape was now overlaid with a totally different nomenclature—old maps were covered in German names for places and geographical features, while newer ones showed the same places with Polish names. Like the Germans, the Poles had lost their eastern territories too, and those who fled from there settled in houses formerly inhabited by Germans in what later became western Poland. To see the post-war period from a Polish perspective was an eye-opener to say the least.

One of my neighbors in Hamburg was an elderly lady born in a small village in the area I was visiting. She had fled across the Baltic ice with her family at the end of the war, and all she had to remind her of the place where she was born was a black-and-white postcard showing the inn which her parents had owned, the schoolhouse, and the lake which flanked the village. I went there during my stay, taking photographs of these places. When I later presented her with a photograph album of the pictures I had taken, she jumped up and hugged me, thrilled at the memories it brought back to her of the home she had left sixty years before. Personal experiences like this motivated me no end in my research into various cultures and languages.

A later trip to Poland took me to Łódź, Warsaw and Kraków. While in Warsaw I saw a book containing photographs of ancient wooden churches, some more than five hundred years old, in the area around Sanok in south-west Poland. So intrigued was I by the images that I went there, hired a mountain bike, and went off in search of some of these charming and slightly other-worldly old churches. The most ancient of them all sits on top of a round wooded hill, has a weathered wooden dome and looks almost like a living creature—a massive brown snail crawling slowly through the woods.

In a garden in one of the villages I visited, I found a greenhouse full of shrubs which had been made from the superstructure of a bus with the undercarriage removed, and I delightedly began taking photographs of it. As I did so a lady came up and started shouting at me. To my mind, the greenhouse was a prime example of the resourcefulness and improvisational skill of the Poles, but she apparently thought I intended to go back home and show people how backward Poland was. By using the best Polish I could muster under the circumstances and uttering some words of praise for her country, I managed not only to stop her shouting but also to change her attitude towards me—afterwards she was falling over herself to help me, excitedly telling me about sights I should on no account miss. For me, experiences of this kind are a striking demonstration of "how to do things with words".

From Polish I moved on to teaching myself Russian, for which it was necessary to learn to read and write all over again. Once I had mastered the Cyrillic alphabet, I found that I already understood a lot of Russian because of the Polish I knew. This was no surprise, of course, as Polish and Russian are both Slavic languages.

A Russian student at Hildesheim University became my informant for Russian, and he was the one who took me to my first-ever church service at an Orthodox church. The church was situated in a suburb of Hildesheim, and as it was Easter according to the Orthodox calendar the service started with a candle-lit procession around the neighborhood. Candle-lit processions again at last! It was just like old times in the Sunday services of the High Anglican church which I had so enjoyed as a child.

During the service, I felt as if the smell of the incense and the sound of the choir were taking me far back in time to a different age. I was touched at the sight of the double-decker metal troughs full of sand and water—the upper one for the living and the lower one for the dead—in which burning beeswax candles were placed. The procedure was to buy a candle, light it, say a prayer over it for a sick friend to get well soon or to commemorate the loss of a loved one, and then plant the burning candle in the sand in the respective trough. My mother having passed away not long before, I felt spiritually uplifted by the blazing candles reflected in the eyes of the people squatting or kneeling by the trough.

My Russian friend invited me to go to Moscow to stay with him and his family in their fifth-floor flat in the center of the capital. Knowing at least the rudiments of the language took me under the surface here too, giving me impressions not usually accessible to tourists. After going to the Tretyakov Gallery and being charged the tourist price when I spoke English, I set myself the task of learning to ask for my ticket in authentic-sounding Russian. This would get me in at the lower prices which Muscovites were charged, I figured, but I didn't do it to save money: it was to see if they would think I was Russian. All day I practiced saying my little piece, and the next morning I nervously took my place in the queue at the entrance. My plan worked and I was overjoyed when I was handed a ticket for the price the "natives" pay. I hoped the huge ladies who tear up the tickets wouldn't ask me any questions and discover that I was an imposter, but they waved me through and I did my best to look Russian as I hurried to see my favourite pictures—baby bears playing in the woods around Moscow, and a view of the watery expanse of the Volga with a tiny Orthodox chapel on a promontory jutting out into it.

My translation studies at Hildesheim University had been more of a vocational training than anything else, and I had not experienced traditional academia or studied advanced linguistics, so I eventually moved to Berlin to study English and Dutch philology. This entailed learning the linguistics as well the language, culture and literature of the English-speaking countries on the one hand and of the Netherlands and its former colonies on the other. My studies of English philology gave me an insight not just into the spatial dimension of the "Other" but into the temporal dimension of it too, and reading Shakespeare and Chaucer was—again—like traveling back in time.

The Dutch are excellent linguists, and people had spoken to me either in English or in German when I lived in Amsterdam, so I hadn't had much of a chance to learn their language. At the Institute of Dutch Philology at the Free University of Berlin, however, the working language was Dutch, and Dutch soon became like a new mother tongue to me. It was engrossing to learn all about Dutch culture, especially in the "Golden Age" of the seventeenth century. It was also interesting to see European history from the viewpoint of the Netherlands, a small country surrounded by powerful neighbors which had been one of England's arch-enemies for many years.

The seventeenth century was, of course, also the century in which members of the Dutch East India Company established a station at the Cape of Good Hope for supplying ships on the way to the East Indies with water and other provisions. As a result of the imperfect learning of Dutch by German, French, Portuguese and other immigrants to southern Africa and of certain processes of pidginization and creolization, seventeenth-century Dutch eventually became Afrikaans.

I applied to participate in a study trip by my institute to Cape Town and Stellenbosch in South Africa and was one of the lucky ones picked to go. Again, music and song helped me to gain an insight into parts of the target culture which usually remain closed to tourists. The first town we visited was Stellenbosch, a stronghold of the Afrikaans language, and one of the most memorable experiences I had there was to take part in a *braai* or barbecue on the roof of the backpackers' hostel in which we lived. I sang songs in Afrikaans, accompanying them on my ukulele, and above us shone the Southern Cross, a constellation I was seeing for the first time in my life. As I sang I noticed that the Orion constellation which my mother had pointed out to me in the heavens so many years before was now no longer standing upright but appeared to be flying almost horizontally across the sky.

Considering the tempestuous history of the southern part of Africa, I was rather unsure as to how politically correct it would be to sing things like *Breng my terug na die ou Transvaal* ("Take me back to the old Transvaal") when we got to Cape

Town. However, my doubts were soon allayed when I met some colored carnival musicians, known as "Cape Coons", at Hout Bay, Cape Town. As I left a boat after a trip to see the seals on the islands out in the bay, the musicians were in the process of playing and singing one of the typical medleys which Afrikaners so like to join in with, and I arrived on the quay just as everyone was singing precisely the song I had had my doubts about. I sang along with them and then I had to hurry to board the tour bus again. If Cape Coons sing it, so can I, I thought. Here, too, I felt as if I had got under the surface of the culture for one fleeting moment. Although I took literally hundreds of photographs during my visit to South Africa, this was the image that stuck in my mind the most and gave me the greatest satisfaction of all.

In my studies of English language and literature, I had learned that, in the three hundred years following the coming of the Normans to Britain, the official language there was French, English being left to its own devices as the spoken vernacular. These three centuries sufficed for English to lose its case markings and start to function in a different way grammatically than its Germanic predecessors had done. It struck me that this was similar to what happened to Dutch in southern Africa seven centuries later: the three hundred years in which Dutch was the official language at the Cape were long enough for the spoken language of the people to develop and change, losing all the old Germanic case markings in the process. The result was a language which now functions in much the same way as English does, encouraging the mixing of the two languages and leading to the rise of a new "super-language" combining both.

Insights of this kind conspired to make me feel I had come full circle. I had often heard it said that "the way to yourself goes halfway round the world," and perhaps that is precisely what happened to me with regard to religion, culture and language. Linguistically, for example: moving to Germany and learning German had been like going back in the history of English to its Germanic roots. Also, my study of Chaucer acquainted me with an earlier form of English which was less strange to me now that I knew German. My knowledge of German grammar also helped me to understand the case system of older forms of the Dutch language, something which contemporary Dutch people have a lot more trouble with, as present-day Dutch has lost most of its case markings.

I feel I have come back home in a moral sense too. When I started out on my forays into the Other, it was not just with the aim of delighting in the immense variety of religious, cultural and linguistic practices to be found throughout the world (though delight in them I did), but also to try and discover for myself some of the basic traits which underlie that variety and unify the contrasts. The principle of reciprocity or The Golden Rule ("Do unto others as you would have them do unto you") is the highest moral imperative of the Spiritualists, and it is also part of the Hippocratic Oath which my mother swore. The realization that the principle of reciprocity is also to be found at the heart of Buddhism, Christianity, Confucianism, Hinduism, Islam, Judaism, Taoism, Zoroastrianism and a host of other traditions has made me appreciate all the more the soundness of this principle, which my mother taught me through actions, not words.

Embracing the Other and making it your own can lead to defamiliarization of what was originally your own, virtually turning *that* into an "Other" and allowing it to be perceived more objectively by comparison with other "Others". I had moved away from my mother tongue and my native culture, and when I returned to them after various forays into other languages, cultures and eras, I found that I comprehended what I had started out with much better than I did before. The experiences of my life showed me that you don't just "have" roots, this attitude being directed towards the past only: you can *take root* in other places too. And taking root elsewhere in turn helps you to understand the roots that you inherited.

On a lighter note, here's one final example of how the things I learned in later life often gave me a new angle on things I learned as a child, presenting me with the wider picture on what I started out with all those years ago. My mother once told me that, if you're nervous about talking to your teacher or some other person of authority, you should imagine them sitting on the toilet. The idea behind this piece of advice was presumably that we're basically all the same, status and authority being man-made and nothing else. She explained that this is precisely what she did when, as a young girl, she was picked to give flowers to the Queen: she imagined that gracious lady sitting on the toilet.

In my English oral competence class at Hildesheim University many years later, my students from Barcelona gave me some intriguing insights into the scatological dimension of Catalonian Christmas customs. These include the *caga tió* or "pooping log", a hollow log which often bears a face at one end and is covered with a blanket to keep it warm. The children "feed" it every day, and when Christmas arrives the log is beaten with a stick, causing it to "poop" out candies and nuts secretly deposited there beforehand by the children's parents.

Not until much later did I learn of the associated Catalonian custom of including a *caganer* (or "pooper") figure in Christmas crib scenes. This is a small figure with its pants around its ankles crouching in a corner of the crib and answering the call of nature. Nowadays these figures are often made to resemble various authority figures and persons of public life, sociologists usually explaining the custom in terms of "defecation as the great leveler".

The pooper figures on sale in 2010 included one of Her Majesty the Queen.

IRAQ 2003: A TALE OF INTERCULTURAL MISUNDERSTANDINGS

BY FRANCIS JARMAN

INDIVIDUAL PEOPLE FROM different cultural backgrounds often find it very difficult to understand and to get along with each other. The same is true of international cooperation in business—with the risk of serious financial consequences—and in politics and diplomacy—with risks that can be far greater.

A recent example of poor intercultural communication is the crisis in Iraq, including the confrontation with Saddam Hussein, the invasion of Iraq in 2003 by a coalition of the United States and its allies, and the turbulence that followed "regime change" (*i.e.*, Saddam's defeat and overthrow). It was not, however, solely the Americans and the Iraqis who failed to comprehend each other properly. Long before any military action was undertaken, the international debate over its appropriateness and legality that took place in the Security Council of the United Nations (and was reflected in international media coverage) showed the representatives of different cultures talking at complete cross purposes. Much of this had to do with differing political positions and arguably also with the at times blatantly nationalistic or self-serving motives of unscrupulous politicians. Yet behind the political conflict and the opportunism it was also apparent that there were genuine differences in the fundamental positions of different cultures *vis-à-vis* what needed to be done about Iraq.

In the following notes, an attempt will be made to explain these differences, and some of the intercultural misunderstandings between the Iraqis and their liberators (or invaders), largely (though not exclusively) in terms of the so-called *cultural dimensions*. Cultural dimensions are one way of describing the different mental programming that exists in different cultures—what Geert Hofstede (1991) has termed the "software of the mind". There are different catalogs of dimensions—Hofstede restricts himself to only five—but I have in recent years chosen to use a broad list of twenty, based not only on Hofstede but also on the work of other intercultural scholars such as Edward T. Hall, Fons Trompenaars and Jürgen Beneke. The list has been published online (Jarman, *Hildesheim Intercultural Film Database*) in the context of an intercultural film project at the University of Hildesheim.

Looking for Weapons

THERE WAS CONSIDERABLE disagreement over how long inspectors should continue looking in Iraq for Saddam Hussein's notorious "weapons of mass destruction" (WMDs). The main players on the opposing sides of this argument happened to come from cultures with very different *time orientations*. With their pronounced emphasis on the here-and-now present and their frequently short-termist attitude to problems, the Americans and the British wanted immediate action and quick results. The French and the Germans, on the other hand, who tend to be oriented slightly more to the future and more inclined to consider longer-term options, saw no reason not to allow the inspectors a more generous time-frame for their work.

The Need for Certainty

IN THE SUMMER of 2003, two eminent European philosophers—the German modernist Jürgen Habermas and the French post-modernist Jacques Derrida, engaging with each other in an unexpected and unprecedented collaboration—published an essay expressing their disapproval of the Iraq War. Their discussion of what they believed was or should be distinctive in European public policy contrasted the "Europeans' trust in the civilizing power of the state", the "ethics of solidarity", the struggle for social justice, and so on, with what they described as the "individualistic ethos of market justice that accepts glaring inequalities as part of the bargain", implicitly: the American way of doing things (Habermas / Derrida, 11).

Members of the Anglo-Saxon cultures do indeed tend to accept a higher level of uncertainty, ambiguity, risk and lack of structure in their lives than Continental Europeans are generally inclined to. In intercultural communication terms, we would say that the Anglo-Saxons are "lower in *uncertainty avoidance*". In the specific case of Iraq, many Europeans, the Germans and the French in particular, wanted clear and unambiguous proof of the existence of WMDs before they would support any use of military sanctions against Saddam's regime. They believed that their governments had adopted a principled position that was morally and legally correct. They were not prepared to act against Saddam without one hundred per cent certainty. Of course, if Saddam had been lying, they were risking political and perhaps military disaster, with catastrophic consequences for the stability of the Middle East and the supply of oil to the West. Even if he had *not* been lying, failing to take action against him would leave in place a vile and murderous regime that was a danger both to Iraq's neighbors (above all, Israel, Kuwait and Iran) and to more than half of Iraq's own population (religious or ethnic groups like the Shia, the Yezidis, the Kurds and the Marsh Arabs, plus anyone who happened to dislike the regime or had the misfortune to displease Saddam or one of his vicious sons). Nevertheless, opinion polls showed that four out of five Germans now believed that Americans could not be trusted (Shawcross 2003, 123) and, when the war began, that a quarter of the French supposedly wanted Saddam to win (155).

In contrast, the Americans and the British were prepared to act on the basis of somewhat controversial evidence and the calculation of probabilities. They adopted a pragmatic position that they believed to be commonsense—if a psychopathic delinquent with a history of violence aims a gun at you, do you wait for him to remove any doubt about his evil intentions by pulling the trigger? Perhaps the direct proof of the existence of WMDs was still missing, but, then again, Saddam in the past had already used them: his cousin Ali Hassan al-Majid (popularly known as "Chemical Ali"), Saddam's usual first choice whenever ruthless brutality was called for, had employed chemical WMDs against Kurdish targets in 1987 and again at Halabja in 1988. On an audiotape from this period which was played at his trial (he was found guilty and executed by hanging in 2010), Ali can be heard telling senior Ba'ath Party officials, in his distinctive, charming style: "I will kill them all [*i.e.*, the Kurds] with chemical weapons! Who is going to say anything? The international community? Fuck them! The international community and those who listen to them" (Human Rights Watch, website).

Saddam may have had a track record of using WMDs, but in the context of 2003 this could be dismissed as circumstantial evidence. In the view of their critics, the Americans and British would by acting precipitately not only be in the wrong but would also run the risk of making a terrible hash of things. Both groups therefore regarded each other's attitude and behavior as irresponsible and morally suspect, and who can honestly say that they were not *both* right?

Loyalty to Saddam

THE INTERACTION BETWEEN the American and British troops and the Iraqis that they encountered also offered huge possibilities for misunderstandings.

If Saddam Hussein were truly such a cruel and oppressive dictator as people asserted, why did so many Iraqis fight for him? And why, especially in the darkest days of the "insurgency" after the invasion, did so many Iraqis apparently yearn for a return to the days of his rule? The first question can only partly be answered by alluding to the loyalty to Saddam shown by members of his Tikriti tribe, who had been given privileged positions in government, the security apparatus and the armed forces, and who sheltered and protected Saddam after his defeat (when he was finally captured, he was cowering in a hole in the ground in a small town just a few miles from Tikrit).

There are two cultural dimensions that may help us Westerners to understand this better. *Individualism/collectivism* considers the comparative importance attached within a culture to the individual person and to the larger group. Members of highly individualistic cultures like the United States, which scored 91 and topped Hofstede's Individualism Index (IDV), or Britain (IDV = 89) may have trouble understanding the attitudes of people in more collectivist cultures like those of the Arab countries (IDV = 38). Saddam could draw upon the support and respect of Iraqis on different levels of collectivity: the Tikritis (as already mentioned); the members of the large, privileged Sunni minority, who had benefited from his rule; and Iraqis in general, whom he had led into war against their neighbors in Iran and Kuwait. It would take time to erode deep-seated feelings of loyalty. In a modern Western culture it would probably suffice to publicize information about the crimes and wrongdoings of the controversial leader—public opinion would then quickly swing against him. Not so in a country like Iraq.

Even more important in this context is the cultural dimension *power distance*, which is about power hierarchies (steeply vertical, or, alternatively, comparatively flat) and the way that cultures tend to deal with inequality. In a high power distance culture like Iraq—the Arab countries scored 80 on Hofstede's PDI Index—there is a significantly different attuitude to authority than there is in low power distances cultures like those of the United States (PDI = 40) and Britain (PDI = 35). In the former, the leader enjoys high status and respect because of who he is. He does not need to demonstrate his competence or expertness, he is obeyed almost unquestioningly, and he is an integrating figure important for the creation of an "in-group" identity. There is a huge social distance between the leader and his followers. In the case of Saddam, the extreme power distance was evidenced by his numerous, sumptuously appointed palaces and the ubiquitous presence of his image in public places in the form of statues and posters. Among the Iraqi population, hatred and fear of Saddam seem to have coexisted with feelings of pride and admiration, a mixture difficult for Americans or Western Europeans to understand, though not for people from other high power distance cultures like, for example, Russia (where Stalin in the days of the Soviet Union had played a similarly hybrid role, simultaneously heroic, avuncular and murderous).

The Americans and British had expected to be welcomed unconditionally as liberators and to be greeted by ecstatic, cheering crowds. It came as something of a shock when—for all kinds of reasons: fear of the foreign invaders, fear of the Ba'athists still amongst them, passivity, resentment of intruders, traumatization—this failed to happen on the scale that was anticipated, and instead soldiers' lives were lost to Ba'athist insurgents. A British battalion commander, Tim Collins (2005), admitting that he'd been naïve, wrote:

> I'd wanted to believe that we'd be greeted as liberators, with crowds throwing garlands. I wanted to think well of the Iraqis. [...] I was going to need to be a little more cautious in my dealings with the locals. [...] I was haunted by my naïvety. I'd been wandering around Al Rumaylah unarmed and seeking to empathize with the locals. Most of them were decent people, of course, but I had failed to look beyond this. I hadn't fully appreciated that there were still those among them who wanted only to regain power and were prepared to kill us, and anyone who cooperated with us, in the process (192).

A few of the liberators unfortunately became embittered about Iraqi ingratitude and contemptuous of the Iraqis, creating an atmosphere that made the abuses at Abu Ghraib prison possible. And some of the Western European opponents of the invasion, forgetting that Iraqis had been freed from one of the most terrifying regimes in modern history—and forgetting also the historical role played by the Americans in liberating Europe from Fascism and then protecting Western Europe from Stalinism—even gave expression to a spiteful *Schadenfreude* that the arrogant Anglo-Saxons should have stumbled so blindly into an enormous trap. Yet the frequently stated view that the liberation of Iraq was wrong, and that Saddam should have been left in place, is in some ways deeply patronizing, even racist. The Iraqis aren't ready for democracy, it insinuates, and their sufferings under Saddam are not a matter of great import! Many Europeans failed to see anything in the invasion of Iraq beyond further evidence to confirm the rightness of their demonization of America (and of the Americans' tame poodle, Britain). It seemed not to worry them that in doing so they were implicitly aligning themselves with the most rabid Middle Eastern enemies of the "Great" and the "Lesser Satan"—with thugs, terrorists and religious totalitarians who are bitterly opposed to the whole Western post-Enlightenment package of social and intellectual freedom.

Doing Business with Friends

IN COMMUNICATION SITUATIONS that are not intensely personal (*i.e.*, involving friends or family), northern Europeans and Americans usually focus—at least initially—on the matter in hand rather than on the human interaction. However, in most other parts of the world (including much of southern and eastern Europe) it is quite different. People there will behave in a *person-* rather than *task-oriented* manner. A business meeting will start with a long drawn out phase of "getting to know you" that will include small talk, the consumption of non-alcoholic beverages, and perhaps also such invitations and entertainments as a visit to the theater or opera, a concert, a tour of the town, an excursion, a restaurant meal, or even (if you are very fortunate) an expensive treat like, say, a geisha evening. The point of all this is to find out who you are and whether you can be trusted, because your hosts prefer to do business with people on the basis of trust and friendship, not contracts. In the film *The Godfather* (directed by Francis Ford Coppola, 1972), the Mafia boss Vito Corleone needs to reach an agreement with his rival and enemy Tattaglia, who, still mistrustful, asks for an additional assurance from Don Corleone. Barzini, the negotiator of the deal, responds with contempt: "Look, we are all reasonable men here. We don't have to give assurances as if we were lawyers!"

American and Middle Eastern ways of working are very different. In the Middle East, where unemployment is often high and labor cheap, there may well be more people working on a job than (to European or American eyes) seems necessary. There will be a high degree of interaction, *i.e.*, they will be intensely aware both of you (and consequently *over*helpful!) and of each other (and therefore particularly concerned with familial and hierarchical relationships), rather than working within the parameters of clearly defined areas of responsibility and quietly "getting on with the job". The "job", in fact, will be seen as inseparable from the people who are involved in it.

In Iraq, the Americans often made the mistake of trying to do things in an efficient, businesslike way, rather than first setting out to win the trust of the local people and *then* working with them, using methods and approaches that the local people understood. After their military victory, the Americans brought in Iraqi politicians who had been in exile under Saddam and who could be "trusted" (it was believed) to work for and with the Americans. But some of these exiles were widely held to be corrupt, and many of them had been away for so long that they were poorly informed and had few contacts in Iraq—and in a collectivist society, networks are everything. Not only were the exiles distrusted by many Iraqis, there was also resentment that the Americans were trying to foist them onto the Iraqi population rather than sitting down with the Iraqis to drink lots of tea, get to know each other, and find out how to restore the battered country to a reasonable working condition.

Even when such meetings *did* occur, the Americans often showed that they lacked the patience and the tact to convince the Iraqis. The US journalist Nir Rosen describes a "council" that they hosted, on June 2nd, 2003, for nearly three hundred tribal leaders from various religious and ethnic groups, who were addressed (in fluent Arabic) by a senior American political advisor, Hume Horan. After Horan had finished speaking, a Shia tribal leader got up and began by expressing his thanks to President Bush for removing Saddam. But then

> [he] asked Horan if the coalition forces in Iraq were liberators or occupiers. Horan responded that they were "somewhere in between occupier and liberator". This was not well received. The tribal leader said that if America was a liberator, then the coalition forces were welcome indefinitely as guests, but that if they were occupiers, then he and his descendants would "die resisting" them. This met with energetic applause from the audience. Several other sheikhs echoed the same sentiment. The meeting deteriorated, and one-third of the audience stood up and walked out, despite the efforts of Horan and other organizers to encourage them to stay (Rosen 2006, 3 f.).

Rosen also describes an angry meeting that took place between two American officers and Mahdi al-Jumeili, the imam of a Baghdad mosque that had supposedly been "defiled" by US troops. At first the outraged cleric is rude and unforthcoming, but after his pride and face have been restored (the meeting is, after all, taking place in the presence of dozens of his congregants) he adopts a much more benevolent tone, explaining graciously that "if America had not occupied Iraq, I would not let you leave without inviting you to my house and shaking your hands. If America leaves Iraq and allows Iraqis to control Iraq, then you would be my friends" (47)—an uncanny echo of the final scene of E. M. Forster's paradigmatic novel about the difficulties of cross-cultural friendship in a colonial situation, *A Passage to India* (1924, 311 f.). The senior US officer quickly (and appropriately) responds by telling him that "if you come to America, you are welcome in my house" (Rosen, 48). It is unclear whether anything substantial is achieved by this particular meeting, but at least an acceptable form of communication has been found.

Don't Stand So Close to Me

WESTERNERS AND ARABS have different attitudes to personal distance and physical closeness. Arabs like to get up closer to people (of the same sex) than most Westerners do, which can be a disturbing experience for many Americans and Britons, and they also seek close-up eye-contact.

In the months after the invasion, US and British troops on the streets of Baghdad, Basra and other cities were involved in countless "incidents", some of which ended in the firing of weapons. Sometimes the soldiers were provoked, spontaneously or deliberately, with abuse or stones, or even fired on out of the crowd by provocateurs intending to cause trouble. But there were also situations where soldiers were unnerved by the *proxemic behavior* of the Iraqis, mistaking their crowding and pushing as a potential attack. It would not have helped that many of the predominantly monochronic Americans, far more linear and ordered in their *time orientation*, would have been irritated by the more polychronic behavior of the Iraqis, especially their tendency to talk simultaneously and not to form queues! The Iraqis for their part must have felt frustrated by the obvious unwillingness of the soldiers to be close to Iraqis, to be touched by them, and to engage in eye-contact. The sunglasses worn by many Americans can only have exacerbated this tension.

God Will Roast Their Stomachs in Hell

A MAJOR OBSTACLE to understanding between Arabs and Westerners is the difference in the role that they assign to *language*. In the West, precision, argumentative clarity and objectivity are emphasized (or so at least we like to believe). In the Middle East, language is valued for enabling the expression of the deepest feelings, and is sometimes not so much a vehicle for conveying thought as a substitute for it—the medium as the message:

> The medium in which the aesthetic feeling of the Arabs is mainly (though not exclusively) expressed is that of words and language—the most seductive, it may be, and certainly the most unstable and even dangerous of all the arts. We know something of the effect of the spoken and written word upon ourselves. But upon the Arab mind the impact of artistic speech is immediate; the words, passing through no filter of logic or reflection which might weaken or deaden their effect, go straight to the head (Gibb 1947, 5).

On the other hand, for all Muslims Arabic is given a unique legitimation—and the spoken version an incomparable glory and resonance—by the circumstance that *this* was the language chosen by God to announce His will to the world, and for the Arab Muslim "every sonorous phrase or inflection [of the Koran] has imaginative associations which are part of his culture and civilization" (Mansfield 1976, 107), enriching and empowering his very being as an Arab. Arabic speakers are consequently far less likely to use their own language, the language of God, ironically, or subject it to analysis, exegesis or deconstruction, than is customary among the sceptical, cynical peoples of the West. Moreover, the fact that most modern Arabs actually have great difficulty understanding the Classical Arabic of the Koran with any degree of precision further encourages what might almost be described as a "romantic" relationship to the language.

"In the Arab world, how you say something is just as important as what you have to say" (Nydell 1996, 117). The public standing of many of the charismatic leaders of the Middle East, from Nasser to Arafat and Gaddafi, has had much to do with their rhetorical skills. Saddam's Information Minister Mohammed Saeed al-Sahhaf frequently made dramatic press conference statements like: "The infidels are committing suicide by the hundreds on the gates of Baghdad! Be assured, Baghdad is safe, protected," "They [*i.e.*, the Americans] are like a snake and we are going to cut it in pieces," "God will roast their stomachs in hell at the hands of Iraqis," or (as US troops could already be seen only a few hundred yards away!) "I triple guarantee you [*sic*], there are no American soldiers in Baghdad." Yet although these pronouncements may sound (to our Western ears) ridiculous and completely detached from reality, it should not be forgotten in what kind of rhetorical context Mr. al-Sahhaf was operating, and what his listeners expected of him.

Hobson-Jobson

IS IT SEEMLY to display your emotions, or not? In the Middle East, *affectivity* (at least by men) is highly valued. The American forces in Iraq often had trouble keeping street demonstrations "under control" and may not always have fully understood the significance that the loud, barely restrained display of emotions in public has for many Iraqis.

The most extreme example (and at the same time a huge security headache for the Americans) is the frenetic Ashura (Muharram) Festival of the Shia, during which thousands of men parade through the streets, shouting and wailing and bloodying themselves with swords and chains, calling out "Ya Hassan! Ya Hussein!" in honour of the martyred grandsons of the Prophet. In the tradition of the great Shia heroes, the young men loudly announce their willingness to endure martyrdom. To outsiders, the whole spectacle may seem both grotesque and disturbing. The British in India turned "Ya Hassan! Ya Hussein!" into "Hobson-Jobson!" This became a mildly contemptuous term for any hysterical-seeming native event and was adopted as the title of the great Anglo-Indian Dictionary of 1886, in which it was defined as "an Anglo-Saxon version of the wailings of the Mahommedans as they beat their breasts in the procession of the Moharram" (Yule / Burnell, 419).

Yet it is somewhat ironic that Americans too have long had a reputation (among northern Europeans) for being almost unpleasantly loud—there is an old joke, from the days when smoking was still permitted on airline flights, in which the lady at the airport check-in desk asks a passenger where he would prefer to sit: "Smoking, Non-Smoking, or Loud American?" For Europeans, this is all connected with the brashness and uncouthness of people from the New World, and is something to be laughed about rather than feared. (Cynics suggest that it is directly linked to American proxemic behavior: if they could bring themselves to stand a bit closer to people they wouldn't have to shout so much.) But to Arabs, who are themselves often very boisterous, this loudness may seem disturbing and even frightening, because it is not always clearly motivated by emotion, as tends to be the case with people from the Middle East. Many Middle Easterners will therefore likely read the loudness of Americans not as affectivity, but as aggressiveness.

The interactive skills of Westerners (and of Americans in particular) frequently leave much to be desired. Charging like the US Cavalry into a complex social environment, bellowing "you guys!" at all and sundry, using first names when talking to near strangers, disrespectfully failing to use academic and professional titles or other indicators of social status, thereby offending against deeply felt views on *formality* and on the respect to be shown towards people of *ascribed* (rather than *achieved) status*, using lewd language in the presence of venerable elders or young women, in general making little effort to adapt or adjust speech and behavior to the expectations of the specific interlocutor—at its most unrestrained, Western behavior suggests a degree of intercultural naïvety tantamount almost to social autism.

THE ANGLO-AMERICAN project in Iraq, should it later be held to have failed, will not have done so because of a complete lack of intercultural good intentions. According to reports in the media, US troops of the 101st Airborne Division deployed to the Middle East in March 2003 were issued with a little handbook providing advice on how to behave when interacting with Iraqis. The soldiers were told, for example: don't try to date Arab women, don't argue the cause of women's rights, don't show people the soles of your feet, don't expect punctuality, and so on (Allison, website). If invited to an Iraqi's home: "Take your leave promptly after the second or third rounds of coffee or tea after the meal." Because: "Arabs socialize and converse before the meal, not after" (Calvert, website). What most guidebooks of this kind fail to mention is that (there always being exceptions to social rules, even in intercultural communication!) you may well be asked to stay longer if they really like you. Though for that to happen, *they* will need to see you as a friendly human being. And *you* will need to work on that.

References

Allison, Wes. "Dispatch from the 101st: There's plenty to learn as war approaches." In: *St. Petersburg Times*, March 12th, 2003. Website, <www.sptimes.com/2003/03/12/Worldandnation/There_s_plenty_to_lea.shtml>

Calvert, Scott. "Army guide offers Iraq do's, don'ts." In: *The Baltimore Sun*, April 29th, 2003. Website, <web.archive.org/web/20030503161548/http://www.sunspot.net/news/printedition/bal-te.journalintro29apr29,0,2164204.column?coll= bal-pe-asection>

Collins, Tim. *Rules of Engagement: A Life in Conflict*. London: Headline, 2005.

Forster, E[dward] M[organ]. *A Passage to India* (1924). London: Book Club Associates, 1987.

Gibb, H[amilton] A[lexander] R[osskeen]. *Modern Trends in Islam* (1947). New York: Octagon Books, 1972.

Habermas, Jürgen / Derrida, Jacques. "February 15, or, What Binds Europeans Together: Plea for a Common Foreign Policy, Beginning in Core Europe." In: *Old Europe, New Europe, Core Europe: Transatlantic Relations after the Iraq War.* Ed. Daniel Levy / Max Pensky / John Torpey. London: Verso, 2005, 3-13.

Hofstede, Geert / Hofstede, Gert Jan. *Cultures and Organizations: Software of the Mind* (1991). Second edition. New York: McGraw-Hill, 2005.

Human Rights Watch. "Chemical Ali in His Own Words: The Ali Hassan Al-Majid Tapes." In: *Human Rights News.* Website, <www.hrw.org/legacy/campaigns/iraq/chemicalali.htm>

Jarman, Francis (Ed.). *Hildesheim Intercultural Film Database.* Website, <www.uni-hildesheim.de/interculturalfilm/index.php>

Mansfield, Peter. *The Arabs* (1976). Revised edition. Harmondsworth, Middx.: Penguin, 1978.

Nydell, Margaret K. (Omar). *Understanding Arabs: A Guide for Westerners.* Second edition. Yarmouth, MN: Intercultural Press, 1996.

Rosen, Nir. *In the Belly of the Green Bird: The Triumph of the Martyrs in Iraq.* New York: Free Press, 2006.

Shawcross, William. *Allies: The US, Britain, Europe and the War in Iraq.* London: Atlantic Books, 2003.

WeLovetheIraqiInformationMinister.com. Website, <www.welovetheiraqiinformationminister.com/#quotes>

Yule, Henry / Burnell, A[rthur] C[oke]. *Hobson-Jobson: The Anglo-Indian Dictionary* (1886). Modern reprint of the 1903 edition, ed. William Crooke. Ware, Herts.: Wordsworth, 1996.

THE DEVELOPMENT OF POLITENESS AS "SOCIAL CURRENCY" IN BRITAIN, THE USA AND BULGARIA

BY EMILIA SLAVOVA

POLITENESS IS ONE of those crucial aspects of communication which facilitate but also often threaten smooth interactions, especially when governed by different cultural norms and expectations. It seems to be "natural" and self-evident, yet it is highly culture-specific, and more apparent when it is absent than when it is present. That is why becoming aware of both your own culture's politeness model and the model of the culture you encounter is crucial in intercultural communication.

Undoubtedly, the most popular metaphor of politeness among linguists in recent years has been that of Brown / Levinson (1987). It regards human interaction as a potential threat to the *face* of speakers; and politeness as a universal "face-saving" mechanism which provides the means for minimizing face threat through the use of a number of hierarchical strategies. The theory has been widely used and discussed, but has also posed a number of problems in intercultural comparisons because of its rather extreme individualistic, universalistic and rationalistic bias.

I prefer a different metaphor of politeness. It draws on Werkhofer's (1992) comparison between politeness and money.

According to this metaphor, politeness is universal in nature, but its manifestations are culturally specific. It is exchanged between individuals, but is socially conditioned. It requires a degree of free will, but is dependent upon a certain sociocultural norm. And while it is based on rationally generated communication strategies, these strategies are dependent upon the conventional politeness strategies functioning within a given language and culture.

Thus, as Werkhofer argues, politeness is neither purely individual, nor social; just like money, it is exchanged between individuals, but is *socially* and *historically* conditioned. Both politeness and money are *symbolic media* whose functions derive from their association with something else, namely *values* (such as social order and social identity). So, Werkhofer maintains, politeness is a social medium which would be meaningless if reduced to the level of the individual; just like money, it relies on the emergence and development of institutions "that define and guarantee what can no longer be interpersonally negotiated" (194).

The parallel with money and economic exchange seems quite adequate and productive; it leads to a metaphorical representation of politeness as *social currency*, which can be further developed and extended. As a social currency, politeness facilitates interactions between individuals, replacing natural economy with a symbolic medium of exchange (the goods for exchange are symbolic too: status, respect, social acceptance). However, while it is exchanged between individuals ("individual politeness"), it is only meaningful as part of a larger system, socially recognized and used by all members of society ("social politeness"). It can be powerful if supported by a strong system of values, or it can quickly be devalued and inflated if those values collapse. When there is relative social stability for a prolonged period of time, the social currency of politeness is also strong, stable and powerful. Frequent changes in power and authority lead to major changes in social order and the related social values and thus undermine the foundations of social politeness.

The metaphor of politeness as social currency correlates with Pierre Bourdieu's view of politeness as *symbolic capital*. In his view, politeness can be seen as a form of *distinction*, a difference, a gap, "that is, a certain quality of bearing and manners, most often considered innate" (1998, 6); a way of setting apart those who are in possession of the latest fashion in behavior and manners from those who, for reason of their more limited access to it, remain behind and can never fully catch up.

The control over what is appropriate verbal social behavior is one aspect of what Bourdieu calls *linguistic capital*. The value of a linguistic performance on the linguistic market is determined not by linguistic competence, but by the laws of price formation specific to that market; and these laws are in the hands of those who have "the power over the mechanism of linguistic price formation" (1993, 80).

It is therefore those in possession of *linguistic capital* who can make the laws of price formation operate to their advantage. This capital gives its proprietors clear dividends: the feeling of being at ease with oneself and one's public behavior, of "being what one ought to be", is one of the direct benefits of the dominant groups' symbolic power (1993, 85). On the contrary, the feelings experienced by the aspirant classes (such as the *petit-bourgeoisie*, in Bourdieu's example) are described as "timidity, tension, hypertension; they always do too much or too little, they are ill at ease with themselves" (*ibid.*).

A look at the socio-historical development of politeness in three cultures, British, American and Bulgarian, can better illustrate this model and lead to insights about intercultural communication. The primary data used are etiquette books and other prescriptive materials. The diachronic perspective seems particularly rewarding, as it reveals how politeness changes with the changing political and economic conditions and the shifts of power distribution in society.

The Development of Politeness in Britain

POLITENESS IS OFTEN stereotypically seen as part of the British national character, and this is not without a reason. Historically, *politeness* developed as a major concept in British culture in the eighteenth century, superseding the medieval terms *courtesy* and *civility* (Whyman 1999). *Courtoisie* (or *courtesy* in English) had originated at court, and referred to manners and behavior at the European courts of the Middle Ages. It gradually receded during the sixteenth century and was replaced by *civilité* (or *civility*), reflecting not the behavior of a particular class but more general human rules of behavior (Elias 1939, Bryson 1998, Burke 2000). Both words remained active in English (though their meaning changed), but in the seventeenth century a new word captured the essence of the time: *politesse* (or *politeness*), and quickly became fashionable in France (the center of the civilized world at the time), from where it spread to other countries. By the eighteeth century it had grown into a dominant ideology in Britain and, as Burke (2000) points out, the term *the culture of politeness* was coined to describe the period.

"Polite" was an adjective used to describe both individual people (with connotations of social superiority) and the exclusive social environment they inhabited ("polite society"), their activities and interests ("polite learning", "polite literature", "polite languages") and their behavior ("polite manners"). The term was used in various collocations to denote refinement, sophistication, attention to ornament and surface forms, elevated learning and the arts, sociability and a range of other positive characteristics. The antonyms of politeness in eighteenth-century thinking were, on the one hand, "vulgarity", "rusticity", "barbarity"; on the other hand, "polite" was opposed to "productive", "useful", "industrious" (Klein 1995). The "polite" were those who devoted themselves to leisure, sports, the ornamental, to fashion and display, and who considered themselves "the Quality" and "the better sort", the gentlemen and ladies of England. In contrast, the "useful part of mankind" were either "industrious" or "business" people (the middling sorts) or the "laborious people" (the lower sort, the common people).

Politeness was a social asset, *symbolic capital* granting access to elite circles ("polite society"). As the 4th Earl of Chesterfield (one of the most ardent proponents of the ideology of politeness in the eighteenth century) wrote, if one wanted to please others and rise in the world, one had to cultivate a complex set of social accomplishments. Politeness was "as necessary to adorn and introduce your intrinsic merit and knowledge as the polish is to the diamond" (*Letters to His Natural Son,* 219). Politeness thus developed into a form of *distinction*. The "distinctive" features of a polite person had more to do with self-presentation than with consideration for others: elegant speech, an agreeable and distinct elocution, good manners and the use of appropriate terms of address, a genteel carriage and graceful motions with the air of a man of fashion, cleanliness and observance of the fashion of the day, "be that what it will", were among the necessary accomplishments providing advancement in society and in the world.

In the course of time, birth began to lose its importance. If courtesy, its predecessor, had originated in the courts and was associated with noble origin, politeness was a natural result of the growing importance of commerce and with it of the middle classes and their need to establish their higher status in accordance with their new role in society (Langford 1992):

> In a sense politeness was a logical consequence of commerce. A feudal society and an agrarian economy were associated with an elaborate code of honor designed to govern relations among the privileged few. Their inferiors could safely be left to languish in brutish ignorance under brutal laws. But a society in which the most vigorous and growing element was a commercial middle class, involved both in production and

consumption, required a more sophisticated means of regulating manners (4).

In spite of the lower status initially attributed to those occupied in business as opposed to those living a life of leisure, it was politeness and manners that helped the newly affluent to establish their upper-class position in society and to attain the status of gentleman. So gradually the meaning of politeness shifted to embrace those "middling sorts", as long as they were ready to invest time and money into acquiring polite manners and the concomitant higher status. Power was no longer dependent solely on origin: it was now commensurate with the economic and symbolic capital owned, and the former often secured the latter: "Gentility without money was embarrassing to all parties. [...] Money without gentility was a commoner butt of humor, but few doubted that possession of it would soon render the possessor polite" (120).

The empowerment of the middle classes in Britain coincided with several key factors towards the turn of the century. What is sometimes known as "the dual revolution", the political in France and the industrial in Britain (Harvie 1993, 470), and the growth of Britain as a colonial power resulted in the growing confidence of the nation in matters of politeness. The demise of the French aristocratic tradition and the growing international power of Britain meant that instead of looking up to France and the French aristocratic salons as the authority on manners and etiquette, as they had done for centuries, British etiquette writers looked inwardly and created their own rules.

By the middle of the nineteenth century, the rituals of etiquette dominated all spheres of public life, and were strictly observed by the majority of the British upper and middle classes (Davidoff 1973, 57 f.). Etiquette and politeness became crucial in structuring social order and social relationships. The period was characterized by a vast number of etiquette books, responding to a growing need for advice on matters of polite conduct. Public behavior was subjected to rigid codification, regulating all major aspects of interpersonal relationships: as Andrew St. George (1993) has noted: "This unwritten social constitution *was* in fact inscribed in the pages of etiquette and manners books" (xiv).

The rules of "Society" exerted powerful control over the life of the individual, and the result was a very strong sense of uniformity, order, predictability, and social cohesion. The only ones who could afford to ignore the iron rules of behavior control exercised by etiquette were social outsiders or those at the very top of society, both of whom could enjoy a more liberal attitude as they did not have to struggle to defend their social position. For all the rest, failing to observe the rules of "Society" carried heavy penalties, accusations of low social origin or poor upbringing, and eventually social ostracism, well illustrated by an excerpt from an etiquette book of a later period:

> Our grandmothers—poor dears—lived their social lives according to an intricate ritual of "do's" and "don'ts", the breaking of any of which led to the terrible accusation of being ill-bred! (Troubridge, *Etiquette and Entertaining,* 1939, 7)

The crux of all rules of polite behavior was keeping a distance. Familiarity was to be avoided at all costs: the well-mannered individual was not familiar, did not intrude on others, ask personal questions, or burden others with personal information (Curtin 1987, 127). Introductions became vitally important in social communication, and no conversation was possible without a proper introduction. Reserve became one of the highly laudable "national" traits. It included the suppression of emotional expression, the composure of face and lack of any animation in the face of extreme circumstances, and the careful guarding of public and private boundaries, or privacy (*ibid.*) Reserve, aloofness, and distancing behavior were a mark of good breeding, while emotional outbursts were considered typical of the lower classes and had to be avoided. Any display of joy, sorrow, or animation was ridiculed by peers and lashed with self-scorn. It was a sign of weakness: immaturity, femininity, or low origin:

> Of course, a true Englishman would naturally regard himself with contempt if he ever permitted himself to look really amiable or pleased. Except in a *tête-à-tête* with a pretty woman, or while enjoying a good game of romps with children, such a thing would be thoroughly bad form. It is one of 'Arry's social mistakes that he grins when he is pleased, or wears a chronic smile if he happens to be a good-tempered man. The men of our class and upwards refrain from any such inane exhibition. (Humphry 1902, 298).

It is worth noting, however, that a significant number of representatives of the lower classes were also subjected to rigid requirements regarding politeness: servants. The close contact with their social superiors required that symbolic distances be doubly reinforced in order to preserve the hierarchy and to uphold the high status of the masters. Indeed, having a large number of servants was one of the hallmarks of being a gentleman. The training of servants was rigorous and exacting. The profession was often passed down from earlier generations, so that the rules of polite and deferential behavior were acquired more or less automatically. The almost inhuman self-control and self-repression were part of the "job description" of the English servant, and were exercised to a high standard:

> They succeed so perfectly in eliminating from their appearance every sign of individuality that it is difficult not to regard them as automata. Their faces are so expressionless, their voices so inanimate, that when one accidentally sees or hears them apart from their calling, it is with a feeling of vague surprise that they are recognized to be as of other men. The soldier

himself is not better drilled than they are (Humphry 1902, 41).

Distance between individuals, as well as between the classes, was ensured by other means too: exclusive gentlemen's clubs, chaperonage of young ladies, and an elaborate system of visiting cards, morning calls and formal visits. All these served the purpose of protecting the individual from "pollution" by inferiors, avoiding unwanted contacts, and maintaining privacy. The "tribal customs of the rich, the well-bred, and the influential developed to a point of baroque ritual" (Victoria Glendinning, introduction to Davidoff, viii) which was impossible for other classes to acquire. This gate-keeping function of etiquette was quite openly acknowledged by etiquette book writers, the arbiters and legislators of social norms at the time:

> Etiquette is the form of law of society enacted and upheld by the more refined classes as a protection and a shield against the intrusion of the vulgar and impertinent, who, having neither worth to recommend them nor discernment to discover their deficiencies, would, unless restrained by some barrier, be continually thrusting themselves into the society of those to whom their presence would be not only unwelcome, but, from difference of sentiment, manners, education, and habits, perfectly hateful and intolerable (*Etiquette for Ladies*, 1863, quoted by Curtin 1987, 130).

The situation gradually started to loosen during the first half of the twentieth century: "The New Etiquette Is Informal", announced the heading of the first chapter of Lady Troubridge's *Etiquette and Entertaining* (1939), while the sub-heading read: "A Different Spirit Has Crept into Those 'Unwritten Laws', and To Be Informal Is Often To Be Correct!" (*ibid.*). Much of the formality and distancing behavior of the nineteenth century gave way to greater informality and more relaxed rules of conduct.

But the greatest change was to take place in the second half of the twentieth century, due to a complex mixture of factors (a world war, Britain's loss of her colonies and then the influx of immigrants from the former colonies; the arrival of television, popular culture, the appearance of youth culture, and the increasing influence of the United States).

> The ideal of a classless society, the growing independence and equality of women, the respect for honesty in speech and social behavior, the general climate of tolerance to what was earlier taboo, and the emphasis on self-expression in individual behavior

were some of the features that would characterize the 1970s, according to *Lady Behave: A Guide to Modern Manners for the 1970s* (1969, xii). With the growing trend for democracy in Europe and the United States, British social and class stratification became suppressed and overt markers of class belonging were mitigated or obliterated.

And even though to this day British society has not become the "classless society" many people in the Sixties and Seventies expected it to become, it has transformed itself and become much more democratic and egalitarian, like many other western societies of recent years. Direct references to differences in class, status and gender have been suppressed, references to "better" and "inferior" people tabooed, and *behavior* betraying feelings of superiority or inferiority is avoided rather than inferior people themselves (Wouters 1995). New groups of previously suppressed people have gained recognition in society, most notably divorced women, single mothers, gays and ethnic minorities. Democracy and equality have become the new values, upheld as the norm, even if often more honored on paper than in reality.

Social etiquette has been gradually replaced by business etiquette, or at least business has been included as one of the major sections in etiquette books (*e.g.*, job interviews). Along with that, the center of power and authority in determining appropriate behavior has clearly shifted away from Britain and in the direction of the United States. This trend is evident in the boom in business etiquette and communication training manuals available on the market. For example, a search in several major British book shops revealed that there were only a few British etiquette manuals available, as opposed to shelves full of guides on better communication, assertiveness training, and similar American-produced or American-influenced issues.

As Cameron (2000a, 2000b) has observed, the trend is largely generated by corporate culture, and etiquette books have been taken over by "how-to-succeed-in-business"-type books. The process has global repercussions, as "[c]ommunication skills training based essentially on mainstream American English discourse norms is [now] spreading around the world" (Cameron 2000b, 41).

Thus *communication skills* seem to be the new candidate for regulating appropriate public behavior, a position once occupied by *politeness*. Communication skills have also become prominent in English language teaching and most conspicuously in business English courses, where effective communication is strongly emphasized. All this clearly follows the shift in political and economic power in the modern world. America has taken over the role of world leader even in matters of etiquette and politeness and is doing it in the form of spreading the ideology of communication skills worldwide.

The Development of Politeness in the United States

IT MAY SEEM that American society is considerably more egalitarian, informal and relaxed in matters of manners and politeness, compared to its British counterpart, but a historical detour will reveal that this was not always the case. The informative introduction to *The Complete Idiot's Guide to Etiquette* (Mitchell / Corr 2000) offers a historical survey of manners and etiquette in America, which will be briefly summarized below.

The pioneers, who came to the New World mostly as outcasts from the Old World, understandably denounced the formalities of the "best" society. The need to establish some order in society was soon felt, however, and the American government began enforcing minimal standards of civility through its laws; advice about proper (and legal) behavior was available from almanacs such as Benjamin Franklin's *Poor Richard's Almanack* (1732-58) or those that George Washington in or around 1748 drew upon for his famous *Rules of Civility & Decent Behavior in Company and Conversation*. With the increase of wealth and leisure in the eighteenth century, the need to acquire more refined manners became apparent, and sources were sought in England's literature on civility. This habit of borrowing printed politeness guides from England continued for some decades after political ties were severed following the American Revolution of 1776. By the 1830s, Americans had started developing their own etiquette books, which were often no less punctilious than their European counterparts. Although manners changed with the times, interest in them remained constant until the middle of the twentieth century. This was drastically changed during the Rebellious Sixties, when "etiquette became a word seldom heard except in jest" (Mitchell / Corr, 8), at least for a while.

Like their British counterparts, American etiquette writers tried to delineate "Best Society" as a club of all those in possession of the symbolic capital of polite and gentle manners, while at the same time trying to diminish the importance of money and birth:

> Thus Best Society is not a fellowship of the wealthy, nor does it seek to exclude those who are not of exalted birth; but it *is* an association of gentle-folk, of which good form in speech, charm of manner, knowledge of the social amenities, and instinctive consideration for the feelings of others, are the credentials by which society the world over recognizes its chosen members (Emily Post, *Etiquette*, 1922).

Nonetheless, the function of polite manners and linguistic expressions as an arbitrary marker of belonging was recognised. They served as a form of distinction between those who had and those who did not have the relevant social and socio-linguistic competence to prove their membership in the club. Politeness and etiquette were thus used not only to ensure social cohesion and harmony, but as a powerful instrument of exclusion:

> People of the fashionable world invariably use certain expressions and instinctively avoid others; therefore when a stranger uses an "avoided" one he proclaims that "he does not belong", exactly as a pretended Freemason gives himself as an "outsider" by giving the wrong "grip"—or whatever it is by which Brother Masons recognize one another (Post, *Etiquette*).

As the confidence of American etiquette writers grew, so the focus of politeness and etiquette shifted from the British and European preoccupation with aristocratic leisure towards the American ideal of business achievement. An English writer on social class saw the difference in the following way: "The purpose of the aristocrat is most emphatically not to work for money" (Mitford 1956, 43), while "Americans relate all effort, all work, and all of life itself to the dollar" (44). An American etiquette guide accounted for the opposition in different terms: social etiquette had been based on the medieval notion of chivalry, while in modern times class hierarchy had given way to corporate hierarchy; the old tradition of giving deference on the basis of gender, age and social caste had been replaced by corporate etiquette, "the dominant force governing modern interpersonal relationships in most parts of America" (Mitchell / Corr, 153).

There has also been a significant change in the power structure of society. The new "best society" is composed mainly of media and show-business celebrities, film stars, and fashion icons, who set the trends in public behavior. Their lifestyle and behavior to a great extent influence the aspirations and behavior patterns of large numbers of people, especially the younger generation (and this influence is felt not only in the United States but on a global scale). Self-presentation and the management of appearance (image-making) are just as important as it was in earlier centuries to put up the appearance of a gentleman. The difference is in the ways this is achieved: friendliness, confidence and self-assertiveness have replaced the preference for distancing and reserve.

All this is directly related to the trend for shortened distances in communication—the growing use of first names, social kissing and the increasing intimacy in public behavior are just some of the markers of this phenomenon (which is discussed in Wouters). The spread of therapeutic discourse has made self-revelation acceptable and even admirable. The previously held view that self-talk was impolite, immodest and vulgar has been replaced by a preference for self-disclosure, assertiveness, openness and the creation of intimacy in public discourse (Cameron 2000a). Preference for directness over indirectness, strategies for minimizing social distance, openness and sincerity have become the new standard for global communication (*ibid.*).

At the same time, many ordinary people are subjected to rigorous training at their jobs, and particularly people involved in the service sector, where there are strict regulations on customer service. This new underclass of people involved in serving others shares a lot of the characteristic features of servants in earlier historical periods discussed above; however, instead of presenting a stern, expressionless and inanimate appearance, they are expected to give a broad smile and be animated and cheerful. ("The smile is included in the price", employees serving at fast-food chains are told.)

Thus there seems to be a clear tendency for shortened distances, increased informality and growing friendliness in communication in American public relationships. However, more informal codes of behavior and feeling cannot necessarily be equated with *easier* codes (Wouters). The new informality is often subject to explicit codification (as in media broadcasts or customer service training). It becomes contrived and formal, even though it should appear spontaneous and relaxed; in fact, "informality is the new formality". It seeks to achieve the appearance of ease, closeness and intimacy, but is subjected to strict regulation, and results in "synthetic personalization" (Fairclough 1989). And even though many people may not perceive any constraint to behave in accordance with the superimposed rules, this new informality is in fact a result of the "constraint to be unconstrained" (Wouters).

In addition, the claims of minority groups to equality create pressure for acceptance and greater tolerance of differences. One result of this is "political correctness", a rather controversial term that covers a range of things like non-discriminatory hiring policies, guidelines for the avoidance of sexist or racist language, and the underlying general change of attitude towards minorities. So along with the greater informality, relaxation of rules, and openness to topics that were tabooed in the past, this imposes new constraints and demands careful monitoring of speech and behavior, not simply out of consideration for others, but because of the existence of clear instructions and strict regulations.

The Development of Politeness in Bulgaria

THERE IS NO doubt that politeness as a social regulator existed in Bulgarian, just as in any other language and culture, long before the word actually entered the language. It made its way into the dictionaries as late as the end of the nineteenth and the beginning of the twentieth century (there are, in fact, three words rather than one, denoting more or less the same: *uchtivost, vezhlivost* and *lyubeznost*; all three being borrowings from Russian). As a popular concept, however, "politeness" has never had the same powerful reverberations in Bulgarian as it did in English—it was never adopted as part of the ideology of dominant groups, nor did it have enough time to develop its own peculiar patterns and norms.

Bulgaria entered the nineteenth century as part of the Ottoman Empire. Its aristocracy had been swept away long before, and with it what patterns of courtly behavior that might previously have existed had also disappeared. There were no state institutions capable of creating and sustaining a standard language, in which certain politeness formulas would be required and gradually become codified. Turkish was the official language of state administration, while Greek was introduced as the language of the church and to a degree also the language of culture and trade. Bulgarian remained the language of everyday contacts within the family and the local community.

Social life revolved around the local community and the extended family. This fact is reflected in the well-developed system of kinship terminology. Kin rather than social hierarchy was essential in interpersonal relationships, and deference was given to old age. There were strict patriarchal discourse norms regulating family relationships; but they were in the form of oral prescriptions, as there were no written etiquette norms available. The great number of spoken proverbs for regulating speech and social interaction attest to the existence of established, even if uncodified, norms, such as "A sweet word opens iron gates", "It's better to have bread and salt with sweet words rather than a big meal with bitter talk", "A good word has no price", *etc*. The first attempt at a written codification of good behavior dates back to 1837, and was a loose translation from the Greek.

After the liberation from Ottoman rule in the late nineteenth century, Western European and Russian influences become apparent. Values, manners, address terms and the polite plural were imported and established in the newly founded state institutions. However, they were used mostly in urban or official settings, while the population at large still preferred the folk terms derived from kinship relations. The tradition of borrowing etiquette and manners chiefly from Western Europe continued until the mid-twentieth century. In the introduction to her etiquette book *Good Manners and Bad* (1938), Olga Radinova clearly states that her work is based on English and French sources, and she often makes comments about Bulgarian royal and social etiquette and outlines the differences with English etiquette.

After the Second World War and the establishment of a new political, social and economic order, etiquette was largely renounced as a bourgeois remnant, and polite manners were considered a marker of anachronistic bourgeois influence. The social forms of address *gospodin, gospozha* (roughly equivalent to "Mr." and "Mrs." and introduced into Bulgarian in the late nineteenth century) were officially replaced with the new forms *drugarko, drugaryu* ("comrade", feminine and masculine forms) in 1948. The terms were a reaction against the class distinctions encoded in the previous forms, and were meant to imply solidarity and social equality. Paradoxically, however, they were often used asymmetrically to persons of greater power as markers of respect.

The most popular etiquette book in that period appears to have been *How to Behave in Society* (1970), a direct translation from Russian (interestingly, the Russian version is itself a translation from Estonian!). The book attaches great importance to the new socialist morality: equality, solidarity, mutual respect, cordiality and benevolence between all people. No purely Bulgarian equivalent seems to be available from that period.

The social circumstances in Bulgaria changed once again after 1989. The old social structures and social order were destroyed, and this is clearly reflected in the rehabilitation of the bourgeois terms of address *gospodin* and *gospozha*. There is also revived interest in etiquette. The appearance of groups of people with new money (the self-proclaimed new elite) brings with it the need for the attainment of symbolic capital in support of the economic kind. As has happened on several occasions in Bulgaria's recent history, the models are chiefly sought abroad and imported without too much adaptation to local conditions.

Politeness patterns are unstable, and heavily dependent on the ever-changing regimes of power and dominant ideologies.

Conclusion

THIS BRIEF HISTORICAL survey of the development of politeness in Britain, the USA and Bulgaria reveals the existence of essential cultural differences which could be productive of different politeness norms and (consequently) of potential problems in intercultural communication.

Historically, politeness in Britain was perceived as a social asset, as a kind of symbolic capital that gave access to elite society (which was appropriately called "polite society"). The development of politeness as a concept and an ideology in Britain coincided with the nation's growth as a colonial power and its rapid economic development after the Industrial Revolution. Politeness norms were no longer imported from the Continent. Britain's growing economic and political power easily translated into symbolic capital, and gave her the confidence to develop her own rules, her own social currency, which could afterwards be exported and disseminated abroad. Politeness developed into a strong national social currency, became part of a powerful national ideology, and was stereotypically associated with British national character. Many of the old rules and norms of politeness are now in the process of dissolution, but they have left a mark on the behavior of people in Britain, even while new standards are being established and promoted.

The comparatively recent growth of the United States into a world power and a global leader is producing similar results. The USA has become less dependent on foreign models of politeness and etiquette and has developed its own approach: "communication skills". Social politeness has lost much of its symbolic power recently, and may sometimes even be regarded with disapproval because of its historical association with elitist discourse and social stratification. There has been a clear shift of emphasis away from aristocratic values and elite culture and towards corporate values and corporate culture. The new ideology of "communication skills" is replacing "politeness" in its function of moulding individuals' behavior on a large scale and its power to grant or prevent access to the professional or social field. Generated by corporate culture, these skills are now being exported to many different parts of the world (including Britain) along with the globalization of business and communications, and the spread of English as a global language.

The long periods of political dependence and instability in Bulgaria did not allow for "politeness" (or any other similar concept) to develop and become established as an independent national social currency. Bulgarian society's system of values was undermined and damaged on several occasions, and so Bulgarians have often looked abroad and imported "manners" and "etiquette". However, because of the constant political changes and reorientation, the models of imitation have often changed too. This has resulted in a lack of stable, widely recognized, uniform standards of socially appropriate behaviour. And while English and American speakers can rely on their accumulated symbolic capital and can revel in the feeling of "being what one ought to be", Bulgarians feel that their symbolic capital is rather scarce and typically exhibit feelings of "timidity, tension, hypertension". Their feelings of uncertainty and insecurity can easily lead to self-marginalization and self-stigmatization. These feelings can be just as harmful to intercultural communication as not being aware of the behavior models typical of the foreign culture.

Studying the politeness norms of the foreign language and culture, the different values, social norms, and historical context, can surely enable a better understanding of other people's interpretive frameworks, as well as help to ward off such dangers as misinterpreting their behavior or causing direct offence. But it is also necessary to develop a critical awareness of your own cultural model and communicative strategies, and to avoid extreme opinions and negative stereotyping of your own culture.

References

Aasamaa, Iina. *Kak da se darzhim v obshtestvoto* ("How to Behave in Society") (1970). Sofia: Naouka i izkustvo, 1978. [Bulgarian text]

Bourdieu, Pierre. *Sociology in Question*. London: Sage, 1993.

------------. *Practical Reason: On the Theory of Action.* Cambridge: Polity Press, 1998.

Brown, Penelope / Levinson, Stephen. *Politeness: Some Universals in Language Usage*. Cambridge: Cambridge University Press, 1987.

Bryson, Anna. *From Courtesy to Civility: Changing Codes of Conduct in Early Modern England*. Oxford: Oxford University Press, 1998.

Burke, Peter. "A Civil Tongue: Language and Politeness in Early Modern Europe." In: *Civil Histories: Essays Presented to Sir Keith Thomas.* Ed. Peter Burke / Brian Harrison / Paul Slack. Oxford: Oxford University Press, 2000, 31-48.

Cameron, Deborah. *Good to Talk?: Living and Working in a Communication Culture*. London: Sage, 2000.

------------. "Good to Talk? The Cultural Politics of 'Communication'." In: *The European English Messenger*, 2000b, 38-42.

Chesterfield, [Philip Dormer Stanhope,] 4th Earl of. *Letters to His Natural Son.* Volume one. Website, <http://books.google.de/books?id=FPPIWkB808IC&printsec=frontcover&dq=earl+of+chesterfield&source=bl&ots=x7JWcA2ejs&sig=GGhou2ANv234pg1zqZi45PoRLOI&hl=de&ei=GrMbTa_HE4y28QPFyK3cBQ&sa=X&oi=book_result&ct=result&resnum=5&ved=0CEYQ6AEwBA#v=onepage&q&f=false>

Curtin, Michael. *Propriety and Position: A Study of Victorian Manners*. New York: Garland, 1987.

Davidoff, Leonore. *The Best Circles: Society, Etiquette and the Season* (1973). With an introduction by Victoria Glendinning. London: The Cresset Library, 1986.

Edwards, Anne / Beyfus, Drusilla. *Lady Behave: A Guide to Modern Manners for the 1970s.* London: Cassell, 1969.

Elias, Norbert. *The Civilizing Process* (1939). Oxford: Basil Blackwell, 1994.

Fairclough, Norman. *Language and Power.* Harlow, Essex: Longman, 1989.

Franklin, Benjamin. *Poor Richard's Almanack* (1732-58). New York: Skyhorse, 2007.

Harvie, Christopher. "Revolution and the Rule of Law." In: *The Oxford History of Britain* (1993). Ed. Kenneth O. Morgan. Revised edition. Oxford: Oxford University Press, 2001, 470-517.

Humphry, Mrs. *Etiquette for Every Day.* London: Grant Richards, 1902.

Langford, Paul. *A Polite and Commercial People: England 1727-1783.* Oxford: Oxford University Press, 1992.

Klein, Lawrence E. "Politeness for Plebes: Consumption and Social Identity in Early Eighteenth-century England." In: *The Consumption of Culture 1600-1800: Image, Object, Text.* Ed. Ann Bermingham / John Brewer. London: Routledge, 1995, 362-82

Mitchell, Mary / Corr, John. *The Complete Idiot's Guide to Etiquette.* Second edition. New York: Alpha, 2000.

Mitford, Nancy. "The English Aristocracy." In: *Noblesse Oblige: An Enquiry into the Identifiable Characteristics of the English Aristocracy* (1956). Ed. Nancy Mitford. Harmondsworth, Middx.: Penguin, 1956, 35-56.

Post, Emily. *Etiquette in Society, in Business, in Politics and at Home.* New York: Funk & Wagnalls, 1922. Also online: Bartleby.com Great Books Online, website, <http://www.bartleby.com/95/>

Radinova, Olga. *Dobri I loshi obnoski: kniga za etiketsiata* ("Good Manners and Bad") (1938). Sofia: Vek 21, 1992. [Bulgarian text]

St. George, Andrew. *The Descent of Manners: Etiquette, Rules and the Victorians.* London: Chatto & Windus, 1993.

Troubridge, Lady Laura. *Etiquette and Entertaining.* London:

Amalgamated Press, 1939.

Washington, George. *Rules of Civility & Decent Behavior in Company and Conversation*. Carlisle, MA: Applewood, 1989.

Werkhofer, Konrad T. "Traditional and Modern Views: The Social Constitution and Power of Politeness." In: *Politeness in Language: Studies in its History, Theory and Practice*. Ed. Richard J. Watts / Sachiko Ide / Konrad Ehlich. Berlin: Mouton de Gruyter, 1992, 155-97.

Whyman, Susan E. *Sociability and Power in Late-Stuart England: The Cultural Worlds of the Verneys 1660-1720*. Oxford: Oxford University Press, 1999.

Wouters, Cas. "Etiquette Books and Emotion Management in the 20th Century: Part One—The Integration of the Social Classes." In: *Journal of Social History*, 1995, 107-24.

POLITENESS PHENOMENA IN ENGLAND, GERMANY AND SPAIN: AN APPROACH TO THE HIDDEN RULES OF BEHAVIOR

BY GUADALUPE RUIZ YEPES

IT IS KNOWN that members of different cultures—and by "culture" I mean "the sum of a social group's patterns of behavior, customs, way of life, ideas, beliefs and values" (Fox 2004, 10)—behave according to different unspoken rules, which develop into patterns of behavior tacitly followed. Most people actually act according to these unwritten rules or behavior patterns of the societies they are part of without being conscious of doing so and without questioning them. Such culture-specific patterns have been studied extensively in the field of intercultural pragmatics (see Sifianou 1992 and Nixdorf 2001, among others), the focus of the research being mainly on the contrastive analysis of how different communities of speakers perform speech acts (see Siebold 2008a). The discipline deals with such discourse conventions as how speakers of different languages open and finish conversations, the function of *small talk* in different cultures, the underlying principles of conversational *turn-taking* and the preferences when it comes to choosing a topic of conversation. According to these studies, communication errors occur because speakers are usually trying to convey their message in the target language by applying rules that are typically used in their mother tongue.

However, intercultural pragmatics is not the only field of study dealing with culture-specific aspects of communication. The Dutch organizational sociologist Geert Hofstede (1991), for instance, is the author of a culture-based classification of communication differences in terms of five cultural dimensions: *Power Distance, Individualism and Collectivism, Masculinity and Femininity, Uncertainty Avoidance,* and *Long- and Short-Term Orientation.* Although it is quite risky to undertake classifications of this kind, because culture is neither homogeneous nor static, but rather heterogeneous and dynamic, and some situations (as we shall see) resist a straightforward, mechanistic analysis, cultural dimensions do often facilitate a better understanding of certain characteristics of intercultural communication. This paper deals firstly with German, Spanish and English behavior regarding the dimension of individualism versus collectivism, and then discusses the differences between these cultures with regard to the speech act of making a request.

Individualism versus Collectivism

BEING BY NATURE very much interested in cultural communication, I have throughout my life slipped unconsciously into the role of an anthropologist. According to Fox, anthropologists

> are trained to use a research method known as "participant observation", which essentially means participating in the life and culture of the people one is studying, to gain a true insider's perspective on their customs and behavior [...] (3).

Since my life has been spent and split mostly between Germany and Spain, I have always compared these two cultures, but I was quite ignorant of English culture. I was expecting the English to be more like Germans, because of their geographical proximity (compared to Spain). But then I came to spend a year in the United Kingdom (Birmingham, West Midlands) working on a post-doctoral project and had the opportunity to discover that it was actually the other way around—English behavior is closer to Spanish than it is to German, at least when it comes to rules of politeness.

In his discussion of individualist and collectivist cultures, Hofstede points out how members of the former are expected to display their individual personalities, thereby defining themselves above and beyond their group affiliations, while in the latter, people usually act as members of a long-term group, such as the family, or an age group.

My experience growing up in Spain and Germany has shown me that Germans normally behave more individualistically than the Spanish do. During a conference in Seville in 2006, I found myself complaining that we had spent most of lunch time deciding where to go for lunch, that is, deciding which restaurant would best satisfy all the members in our group. There were eight of us! As I pointed out to my German colleague, in Germany the problem would have been solved very quickly! The people in the group wishing to go to the Chinese restaurant would have done so, the people wanting to go to the Italian would have done so too, and so on. The group would have split, but everyone would have got what they wanted. Nor would it have been unbearably traumatic to have split up for lunch, as we would be seeing each other anyway during the following sessions of the conference, and were also planning to have dinner together that evening. The response of my German colleague was that I had become *germanized*, as he put it. And he was probably right. In a collectivist culture, such as Spain, the members of a group will usually try to find a harmonious solution to conflicts, and it would be seen as impolite and selfish to suggest that everyone might go to different restaurants. In an individualist culture, like Germany, it would be the most natural thing in the world to split the group, since we would be seeing each other again anyway after lunch.

As already mentioned, I was expecting English people to be more like the Germans—after all, Great Britain is near the top of Hofstede's Individualism Index, way ahead of Germany—but after observing them day-to-day in their natural habitat I realized that, in certain respects at least, they had much more in common with the Spanish than I would ever have thought. I attended many conferences in the United Kingdom and realized that, just like the Spanish, English people (maybe the British in general) often tried to find solutions that would satisfy everyone rather than suggesting splitting the group. What could be the reason for that? Were considerations of politeness (or fair play) perhaps trumping natural Anglo-Saxon individualism?

The English and Spanish are also similar—and different to the Germans—in the way that people buy their drinks in the pub. When a group of friends go out together in Germany, everyone pays for his or her own drinks and food (what in English is called "going Dutch"). The Spanish/English way is for everyone in turn to buy a round when they go out to a pub for a drink, which means that the slower drinker tends to end up with a little collection of untouched beers! As to eating at a restaurant with a group of friends, Spaniards usually divide the bill equally between the diners, so that everyone pays the same amount regardless of what they ate or drank; Germans, in contrast, will only pay for what they ordered. When I was an undergraduate at the University of Granada, I remember one night going to a restaurant with my fellow students of the international business module. We were about eight Spaniards and one exchange student from Austria. When the bill came and it became clear to the Austrian that we were going to split it into equal parts, he complained and said that he would have ordered something more expensive had he known that! We decided that he would pay only for what he had ordered, and the rest of us divided up the remainder of the bill.

Politeness Rules in the Speech Act of Making a Request

IN INTERCULTURAL PRAGMATICS there has been a growing interest in the contrastive analysis of different language combinations, English being the most analysed language of all. Sifianou (1992) and Nixdorf (2001), for instance, take the English language as a starting point and contrast it with other languages. Studies comparing German and Spanish are quite rare, though, and studies comparing German, Spanish and English even more so. One of the first authors to carry out a study in German and Spanish intercultural pragmatics was Keim (1994). She looked at intercultural interference in German-Spanish business communication and discovered that Germans and Spaniards are very different in the way that they handle turn-taking. Whereas Spaniards tend to interrupt each other in conversations very often and the overlapping can last quite long, Germans interrupt each other less and the periods of overlap are shorter, since the speakers end up giving way to each other.

Another example of research in German-Spanish intercultural pragmatics is Siebold's studies in the field of speech acts (2008b). She analyzed a corpus of 126 filmed and transcribed Spanish-Spanish and German-German everyday life role-plays and compared them in terms of speech acts of apology, request, compliment and compliment response. In this paper we shall extend her study regarding the speech act of making a request by including English-English everyday life role-plays. As Siebold explains (2008a, 11), Spanish people use direct strategies such as an imperative (example 1) or direct questions (example 2) in order to express a request, while Germans tend to use indirect strategies such as uttering a wish (example 3) or asking the recipient (example 4) whether he or she feels capable of meeting the request.

Example 1: *Niña, dame cinco croissants y una barrita, anda.*
Example 2: *Hola Señora, buenas tardes, mire, busco el Corte Inglés, me han dicho que está en la calle Luis Montoto, ¿está*

lejos?

Example 3: *Ich hätte gern fünf Croissants und ein Baguette, bitte.*

Example 4: *Ach, entschuldigen Sie bitte. Ich kenne mich hier überhaupt nicht aus und ich möchte so gern zum Marienplatz. Könnten Sie mir vielleicht mal sagen, wie ich dahin komme?*

The strategy preferred by Spanish speakers involves interfering directly in the *terrain* of the recipient, which is softened by the use of affectionate forms such as *niña* (example 1), interpersonal markers such as *anda* (example 1) or politeness markers such as *hola señora, buenas tardes* and *mire* (example 2). These forms are used to compensate for the speaker's intrusive directness/use of the imperative, creating a pleasant atmosphere and feeling of social proximity between the two interlocutors. In the German dialogues, it is clear that very different strategies are in play. They are not used to interfere directly in the *terrain* of the recipient, and distance is maintained by means of the subjunctive mode of the verb, like *Könnten* (example 4), or other politeness forms, like *bitte* (example 3), *mal* and *vielleicht* (example 4).

Now, what about the English? Are they direct like the Spaniards or distant like the Germans? My experience during the time that I spent in the United Kingdom has taught me that they use much the same strategies as those employed by the Spanish.

Example 5: *Ticket!* [The ticket is handed over to the bus driver] *Thank you love!*

This role play took place in Birmingham's central bus station between a bus driver of the National Express coach company and myself. It happened at the very beginning of my stay in England and I was very surprised to be called "love" by a complete stranger. But I got used to it quickly, when I realized that it wasn't a habit of that particular bus driver alone—the cashiers at Tesco's and other grocery stores also made use of this kind of affectionate expression. It has to be stressed, though, that their use is, in my experience, more typical of people of a certain age—the bus driver as well as the cashiers using these expressions were at least fifty years old. The same can be observed in Spain, since expressions like *niña* and the like are typically used by elderly people.

This kind of behavior reminded me of the folks in Milwaukee, WI, where I spent a year teaching German and Translation Theory at the University of Wisconsin-Milwaukee. In contrast to the Spanish and English habits, I observed that affectionate expressions in the USA are used by all age groups, with "honey" being a particular favorite. As for the Germans, as already mentioned they prefer to use syntactical structures that maintain with their "correctness" the appropriate distance, instead of transgressing politeness by using a direct imperative and compensating for this transgression by using terms of affection.

Conclusions

THE OBJECT OF this paper has been to compare some of the unwritten rules of behavior that help to define our national identity and character. Looking at the Spanish, the Germans and the English, we see that their cultures are distinctive and unique. We can agree with George Orwell (1941) when he declares that cultural identity is something "continuous, [that] stretches into the future and the past" (2142). Societies develop very quickly and social behavior is, therefore, constantly changing, but there are particular features of national identities that persist over the course of time. As Orwell says:

> What can the England of 1940 have in common with the England of 1840? But then, what have you in common with the child of five whose photograph your mother keeps on the mantelpiece? Nothing, except that you happen to be the same person (*ibid.*).

The same could be said for German or for Spanish culture. We could continue comparing rules of behavior in other aspects of everyday life, in humor, pub-talk, the rules of the road, dress codes and so on, and we would end up with a kind of "grammar" of Englishness, Spanishness or Germanness, but this would be far beyond the scope of this short essay.

I hope to have shed a little bit of light on some of the differences in behavior between these three cultures, so that if you happen to visit any of these countries, you will not feel completely lost, but be better able to behave according to the German saying: "Andere Länder, andere Sitten!" ("Other countries, other customs!"). Or its English and Spanish equivalents: "When in Rome, do as the Romans do!" and "Donde fueres, haz lo que vieres" ("Wherever you go, do as you see").

References

Fox, Kate. *Watching the English: The Hidden Rules of English Behavior.* London: Hodder and Stoughton, 2004.

Hofstede, Geert / Hofstede, Gert Jan. *Cultures and Organizations: Software of the Mind* (1991). Second edition. New York: McGraw-Hill, 2005.

Keim, Lucrecia. *Interkulturelle Interferenzen in der deutschspanischen Wirtschaftskommunikation.* Frankfurt/M.: Peter Lang, 1994.

Nixdorf, Nina. *Höflichkeit im Englischen, Deutschen, Russischen: Ein interkultureller Vergleich am Beispiel von Ablehnungen und Komplimenterwiderungen.* Marburg: Tectum Verlag, 2001.

Orwell, George. "England Your England" (1941). In: *The Oxford Anthology of English Literature. Vol. II.* Ed. Harold Bloom / Lionel Trilling / Frank Kermode / John Hollander. New York: Oxford University Press, 1973, 2141-60.

Siebold, Kathrin. "Die interkulturelle Pragmatik: Angenehm, sie kennenzulernen!" In: *Magazin,* 18, 2008a, 8-13.

------------. *Actos de habla y cortesía verbal en español*

y en alemán: Estudio pragmalingüístico e intercultural. Frankfurt/M.: Peter Lang, 2008.

Sifianou, Maira. *Politeness Phenomena in England and Greece: A Cross Cultural Perspective.* Oxford: Clarendon Press, 1992.

CONFLICT OVER LAUNDRY: THE CULTURE OF WASHING IN GERMANY AND SWEDEN

BY ANNE-KRISTIN LANGNER

"Culture is conflict over meaning."
—Ben Agger

IT WAS A NORMAL Sunday some time in the summer, in a little village in the north of Germany. The weather was sunny and windy enough to dry one's laundry outside, in the garden, on the terrace, or on the balcony. A Swedish woman who had moved to Germany a short while before had exactly this idea. Living in a small apartment in an apartment block, with many neighbors living around her, she decided to use the small space of her balcony to dry the laundry. She couldn't think of anything wrong with that, and was therefore surprised when her neighbors reacted to her laundry activity with considerable interest, even annoyance. When her husband, a German police officer naturally familiar with German laws and social rules, came home he was quite shocked, and said that hanging your laundry outside on a Sunday was simply not done in Germany. Even the use of the clothes washer was problematic, since it might disturb the neighbors' Sunday rest.

The Swedish woman didn't understand a word. Having

grown up in Sweden and having spent most of her life there, she assumed that doing laundry on a Sunday was perfectly acceptable. The reason is simple and comprehensible. Sunday is for many Swedes (just as it is for Germans, too) the only day of the week that is completely free. No work, no stress—a perfect day to do all the household things (including laundry) for which there is no time during the week when everybody is working. And why should people get excited over their neighbors' laundry? But it is a different story in Germany. Every federal state in Germany has its own legislation regarding approved activities on Sundays or public holidays. In most cases, making a noise is strictly forbidden on days like these. One might argue that pegging out the washing hardly makes much noise. But the clothes washer can be a different matter altogether. On top of this, it may also be the case that the landlord's house rules prohibit the hanging out of laundry to dry. Rules, rules, and regulations... There are internet discussion forums devoted to the question of what is allowed on a Sunday and what isn't. Who really knows?

Nor should one forget that in Germany noise is also not allowed during the early afternoon—another thing that caused the Swedish woman no little stress during her first month in Germany. Because after having given up the idea of doing the laundry on a Sunday, she switched to weekdays. During that first month, she spent most of her time at home, to get used to life in Germany and to prepare herself for the program of studies that she was planning to undertake. There was therefore no problem (as she saw it) getting the laundry done on a weekday. Unfortunately, she chose the wrong time, 2 o'clock in the afternoon, in the middle of the German siesta, which house rules often define as lasting from 12 noon to 3 o'clock. She was also unlucky in that in her block of flats there were precisely such rules. Once again her husband was shocked to find her washing the clothes. "Did you switch on the clothes washer? You can't do that!" Her shocked reaction was that the clothes washer must be broken and that she shouldn't have switched it on—until her husband pointed out that the clothes washer was fine, *but* that she was disturbing the peace of the siesta.

WHAT IS GOING on here? This funny but true story makes me think of the intercultural differences between Germany and Sweden, differences which you wouldn't necessarily expect. The two countries are geographically very close, and that has often made people believe that Germans and Swedes must share the same attitudes and values. But the experience of a culture that you expect to be similar to your own is often much more turbulent than that of a culture that is obviously exotic, as, for example, in the interaction between Germans and Asians. This *faux ami* frequently leads to misunderstandings and conflicts between cultures. In the case of our little laundry problem, there are several cultural traits that, let's say, separate Germans from Swedes when it comes to washing clothes.

Talking about cultural traits involves recognizing the idea of categorizing cultural specifics, so as to be able to explain and compare certain phenomena. Culture, in this context, can be seen as a common base of ideals, values and attitudes that you at least partly share with other people from your social environment. Some are obvious and, taking the iceberg as a metaphor, move about on the surface, visible to everybody—architecture, the way people dress, food, generally speaking, things that are easy to observe and to measure. Under the surface, though, is the lower part of the iceberg, cultural ideas that are hard to observe and to measure and often invisible to people. They include, for instance, customs, personal space, or matters of education.

Regarding culture as a kind of "collective programming" (Hofstede / Hofstede 1991, 4) that leads to a common base of values and attitudes, which both connect people but also distinguish a group of people from other groups, is one possible definition of culture. The term is ambiguous and with literally hundreds of definitions in circulation, positively dangerous. Culture is often used to describe works of art, for instance, which means it is used in an aesthetic or textual context, but also to describe patterns of human behavior, as is done by anthropologists.

Defining culture as a social phenomenon is more appropriate for our purposes. However, this alone will not solve our laundry problem. To do this, we need to look below the surface, at the hidden part of the cultural iceberg, at certain customs and values. Various approaches have been developed to help us discover, analyze and compare these invisible cultural traits. That this was possible is due at least partly to the work of cultural anthropologists like Margaret Mead and Ruth Benedict, who discovered, as the Hofstedes have put it (22), that "all societies, modern or traditional, face the same basic problems—only the answers differ". From this basic and essential starting point, Amercian social scientists of the mid-twentieth century began to work on the idea of culture and its classification. For example, Talcott Parsons described culture as an essential part of the social system of every society and used cultural patterns to describe the structure of the social system (1951). The cultural anthropologist Edward T. Hall is often said to have been the main inspiration behind "cultural standards" and "cultural dimensions". In *The Silent Language* (1959), he analyzed the significance of nonverbal communication for intercultural interaction. *The Hidden Dimension* (1966) discusses the interdependence of culture and how the personal understanding of space impacts on the architecture of a country. How time is experienced differently from culture to culture is explained in *The Dance of Life* (1983). Confirming a popular cliché, people from the warmer south are found to be much more relaxed and to not suffer so much from deadline constraints as do people from, say, England or Sweden. And *Beyond Culture* (1976) can be seen as an appeal to people to break through cultural barriers and to discover cultural diversity.

One of the best-known representatives of the idea of explaining cultural differences through "cultural dimensions" is the Dutchman Geert Hofstede. His emphasis is on national cultures and his approach derives from the business world and from organizational psychology. Hofstede found a way to show *how* and *why* cultures differ (or correlate). His huge study of IBM employees in 66 different countries produced a focus on five cultural dimensions: *Power Distance, Individualism and Collectivism, Masculinity and Femininity, Uncertainty Avoidance,* and *Long- and Short-Term Orientation.* Hofstede applied the dimensions not only to business but to society in general—to the family, the school, the state, and to organizations. In Germany, power is distributed fairly equally, so that students don't hesitate to speak up in class, even to the point of contradicting what their professor has just said; and the individualistic orientation in Germany encourages people to speak up, presenting and defending a personal opinion. It is also acceptable, in a "masculine" culture like Germany, to strive for career success. Sweden is said to be individualistic, too, but it has a strikingly "feminine" cultural focus that is reflected in the numerous clubs and associations that bring people together and help to establish good relationships.

CULTURE IS NOT a rigid, static thing. People might belong to a certain national culture, like the French or Norwegian culture, but to several subcultures as well. A subculture could be, for instance, a certain job culture, depending on one's occupation. If you work in a garage, the atmosphere and ways of communicating will be totally different to those in a university. Every time a person changes their job, the job culture in the new working environment is likely to be different. It is the same with interests and hobbies. Joining a sports club exposes the member to the written and unwritten rules of the sports club culture. Therefore one does not belong to one enclosed culture, but to a cultural mix that may quickly change in its composition.

It is the same with the cultural dimensions. They are not closed entities that simply coexist next to each other, but they correlate in different ways creating a unique and living national culture. For example, the Swedes score very high on Hofstede's Individualism Index, but at the same time they are the most "feminine" of all the cultures in Hofstede's study. How does *that* go together, one might ask—being highly individualistic and modest simultaneously? Well, individualism for Swedes means that they are independent and that they enjoy "the freedom to be" (Robinowitz / Carr 2001, 58)—to be independent from others. A teenager moving out of their parents' home at the age of sixteen is normal, desired and supported by the Swedish welfare system, which aims to offer equally good chances to everybody. The ideal would even be for *every* teenager to move out at the age of sixteen, so that everybody could be independent and self-sufficient without anyone having substantially more than others—an appeal to the "feminine", egalitarian side of Swedish society. This is one reason why Swedes love gambling, because it strikes both an individualistic and a "feminine" chord. A game that is only based on people's luck offers the same chance for everyone and so if somebody becomes more independent due to the fact that he or she has won a large amount of money *by luck*, then that is quite all right for a Swede. By the way, when you are in Sweden, keep your eyes open for places where you can gamble—you'll find quite a lot of them.

It is much easier with Germans, though. That they are both individualistic and "masculine" means that they can strive actively for achievement and success, which will be accepted so long as it is not destructive of other people's chances. Whereas the Swedes are more passive in showing their independence, the Germans actively proclaim their individualistic wants and needs. If you can afford to buy a bigger car than your neighbor, do it, there is nothing wrong with that, quite the contrary in fact, since your behavior reveals what you want and what your personality is like. Showing your character, the thing that distinguishes you from others and is the face that you present to the world, appeals to the individualistic and "masculine" German mindset. Germans love to fight for their rights, and show who they are, and they do not eschew conflict, so beware! There is a well-known television show in Germany, *Schlag den Raab* (the

English version is called *Beat the Star*), in which the contestants have the chance to win millions if they can beat their host Stefan Raab overall in a game covering fifteen different disciplines, ranging from extreme sports to chess. In the end, someone wins the huge jackpot, but some contestants walk away with nothing but a bloody nose.

Schlag den Raab may have a lot to do with German individualism and "masculinity", but with regard to the Swedish woman and her German laundry problem we need to turn to the cultural dimension of Uncertainty Avoidance. Germany is known worldwide as an "over-regulated" country, where everybody is always on time and where people strive for perfection. In short, Germans try to avoid uncertainties whenever and wherever possible. This is the case with the woman's German husband. As a police officer, his job is to enforce the rules and regulations and to be on the lookout for people ignoring them. Although laundry on a balcony on a Sunday is not a strict law (anymore), he knows how deeply rooted these rules are, and doesn't want to have arguments with the neighbors, which might create further uncertainty along the lines of "What'll happen if the neighbor talks to the landlord then?" My grandmother once told me that every Sunday that I washed my clothes, somebody was going to die because I wasn't keeping to the rules. That was weird. And it heightened my personal feeling of uncertainty quite considerably. So laundry in Germany is not a personal decision, because you need to keep to certain rules so as not to destroy your neighbor's everyday routine and, as a consequence, leave them with a feeling of irritation and uncertainty. And then it is not a matter of privacy anymore.

As with all cultural traits, the degree of uncertainty one has to live with is not innate, but learned. My grandmother's stricture is just one very specific example. A more general one is connected with the use of technology in Germany. The instruction sheets delivered with every piece of technology are usually very long and detailed, including pictures with arrows and hardly any repetition in the text in order not to create any misunderstandings. People are strongly encouraged to read the instruction sheet thoroughly before the piece of technology is put into operation. The expertise invested in technological development is an example of high uncertainty avoidance. The higher the supposed level of expertise and the better and longer the training of the design engineers and technicians, the safer and better the product is held to be. Feeling uncertain in particular situations can lead to a higher degree of aggressiveness than in low uncertainty avoidance cultures. Taking this into account, one can understand why the woman's husband and the neighbors reacted to her behaviour in an unfriendly and humorless way.

In contrast, aggressive and emotional behavior is not a Swedish thing, since the Swedish idea of uncertainty and privacy is different. To begin with, for many Swedes there is no need to feel uncertain in any way. Sweden has an efficient social welfare system, which is often called *Moder Svea* (Mother Sweden) and which looks after everybody. Since the Thirties, Sweden has been known as *folkhemmet* ("the home of the people") (Robinowitz / Carr, 20), which offers egalitarian living conditions for everybody, meaning, for instance, that only a few people are unemployed even during an economic crisis and that the tax levels for rich people are high in order to balance out their income with the salaries of average wage earners. So there is no need to be uncertain, to worry about tomorrow or to react peevishly towards others (whose chances are no better or worse than yours). Within Sweden's egalitarian and homogeneous society, people make a great effort not to get involved in conflict. The "feminine" Swedes strive for harmony and are strongly "dependent upon surrounding views and attitudes and upon having good relations [...]. [They] emphasize the social surroundings and friendly atmosphere" (Daun 1996, 73). That is why you would just ignore the neighbor's laundry, even if it annoyed you a bit. It's typical for a Swede not to make a fuss, but to look for a good consensus or even change the topic if necessary. Or barricade yourself within your private space if the relationship might actually suffer if you spoke up. Laundry is not something a Swede would make a fuss about, and not something for which you would risk endangering a friendship.

In Sweden, your private life and harmony are often strictly separated from public life. Forced to choose between *ensamhet* (loneliness) and *gemenskap* (community), a Swede would probably go with *ensamhet*. As Daun emphazises (71), there is a strong need for independence. To protect your private space and independence from others, it is, for example, unusual to start a business meeting with small talk about hobbies, children or holidays. It is common in Sweden to share private things only with the immediate family and your closest relatives. Daun gives a vivid example of the strict division of private and public life:

> Seemingly meaningless aspects of Swedish culture can be seen in the light of this border between private and public: for example, the custom of thanking the hosts for a nice evening *before one dons one's coat and hat*—something that astonishes many foreigners. As long as the guests do not have their coats on, they are totally within the hosts' private sphere. It is with intimacy—a quality of the private sphere—that farewells should be exchanged. Outer garments—hats, coats, and so forth—are symbols of the public space in which they are used (72, emphasis in the original).

That a Swede will accept and respect other people's laundry routines should be obvious now; it is a matter of individual privacy and has nothing to do with public life. Rules are unnecessary. The Swedish social system is regulation enough and keeps uncertainties to a minimum.

The Swedish sense of independence and tolerance towards others leads us to another point that could help us to understand what was going on with the Swedish woman—religion. The historical and religious significance of Sunday in Germany is that this day should be free and different to the other six days of the week. The church and especially the Christians tried to protect Sunday and to keep it free of any kind of work. Sunday is in some ways an institutional matter for the church. Religion in Sweden, on the other hand, is less connected with the church as an institution. What is more important is respect for others and a spirituality that need not necessarily have anything to do with the church. A church-regulated Sunday does not fit in with the idea that Swedes are independent of others and that nobody is above anyone else—*pares inter pares*. Nobody should be telling you what to do, especially not in your private space and time.

The same applies to management in Sweden, as Susanne Müller (2005) has explained (152). The Swedes have a very egalitarian way of doing business, which means that it is not the boss but the team as a whole which decides what to do: the hierarchical structures are flat. This is strongly related to the *Jantelagen*, an unwritten pattern of rules and behavior that was elucidated by Aksel Sandemose in 1933. In his novel *En flyktning krysser sitt spor* (*A fugitive crosses his tracks*) Sandemose formulates ten rules of behavior while describing the life in a small Danish town called Jante. The rules say that nobody is above or better than others, and that everybody is supposed to be the same. Although the *Jantelagen* is a negative expression of small town mentality, is is deeply rooted in the way that the Swedes live together. So—nobody would feel superior enough to tell you when it's your laundry time.

In contrast to the Swedes, Müller describes the Germans as being more target-oriented (235). Reaching a consensus is much less important than achieving an economically significant goal. With regard to the idea of "masculinity" and "femininity" in Germany, discussions are allowed and encouraged yet it is perfectly acceptable for one person to be above the other as long as the best solution is found—and hierarchical structures are often seen as playing an important role in the business of finding the best solution to the problem. At the same time, though, Germans are said to be team-oriented, since the goals are discussed, team communication is encouraged and tasks are shared.

Laundry and the whole process around it mean different things in Germany and Sweden, embodying ideas and values that are rooted deep within the two different cultures. When Germans and Swedes meet over the washing, there may be misunderstandings and conflict. Culture is present even in the smallest matters, things that are not regarded as especially important—such as the laundry. Whereas as a Swede might think "Sköt dig själv och skit i andra" ("Look after yourself and don't worry about the others"), laundry for Germans can be and often is a place for public discussion. There is no "better" or "worse" and no value judgement here, but simply a difference in meaning.

REFERENCES

Agger, Ben. *Cultural Studies and Critical Theory.* London: Falmer Press, 1992.

Daun, Åke. *Swedish Mentality* (1996). University Park, PA: Pennsylvania State University Press, 2002.

Hall, Edward T. *Beyond Culture* (1976). New York: Anchor Books, 1981.

------------. *The Silent Language* (1959). New York: Anchor Books, 1981.

------------. *The Hidden Dimension* (1966). New York: Anchor Books, 1982.

------------. *The Dance of Life: The Other Dimension of Time.* New York: Anchor Books, 1983.

Hofstede, Geert / Hofstede, Gert Jan. *Cultures and Organizations: Software of the Mind* (1991). Second edition. New York: McGraw-Hill, 2005.

Müller, Susanne. *Management in Europa: Interkulturelle Kommunikation und Kooperation in den Ländern der EU.* Frankfurt/M.: Campus, 2005

Robinowitz, Christina Johansson / Carr, Lisa Werner. *Modern-Day Vikings: A Practical Guide to Interacting with the Swedes.* Yarmouth, MN: Intercultural Press, 2001.

Parsons, Talcott. *The Social System.* London: Routledge & Kegan Paul, 1951.

Sandemose, Aksel. *A Fugitive Crosses his Tracks* [*En flyktning krysser sitt spor*, 1933]. Transl. Eugene Gay-Tifft. New York: Knopf, 1936.

THE FRENCH PLAY OF SEDUCTION

BY ISABELLE KROSS

PLAYING WITH LANGUAGE occurs in all languages and in all cultures. People play with their language in idioms and metaphors like "chair *leg*", or in proverbs like "to cost an *arm* and a *leg*", but these are not necessarily used consciously. The objective of this article is to observe the intentional and active play with language in French culture. Three elements are necessary for such play: the play itself, the players, and the appropriate rules:

The play=the language
The players=the speaker and the hearer(s)
The rules=the communication modi

(Note: I have preferred "play" to the more idiomatic noun "game" because the former so nicely includes the *ludic* and *theatrical* elements of what I shall be describing, as well as the idea of an *intended strategic move*.)

The Play

THE FRENCH LANGUAGE offers, especially in its spoken form, optimal conditions for language play. In English, for example, the spelling of "saw" can mean two different things, *i.e.*, a tool for carpenters, or the past tense of the verb "to see". But this homophonic phenomenon is not restricted to such cases with identical spelling and identical sound used for different meanings, but also includes cases like "meat" and "meet", which are not spelled in the same way and have different meanings but identical sounds.

In French, the phenomenon of homophony appears in spoken language very frequently; it is not limited to the word level, but is already present at the level of the letter, like for example the vowel *o*, pronounced [o]. This one letter can have the meanings of "water" (*eau*), (pl. *eaux*), "high" (*haut*), (pl. *hauts*), "to" (*au*), (pl. *aux*), or the exclamation "oh" (*oh*). Following the letter, the next level is the syllable, which offers many opportunities for homophonic combination, like [po]: "skin" (*peau*), (pl. *peaux*), "pot" (*pot*), (pl. *pots*), or "chance" (coll., *pot*). If we put one consonant more at the end of the syllable, we can still have homophones, like the sound that can mean "pig" (*porc*), "harbor" (*port*), "postage" or "carriage" (*port*), "wearing" (*port*), and so on. And then there is the phenomenon of paronyms, for example "I saw/eyesore". Continuing in that vein, if we just change the consonant, we can move from [po], "chance" (coll., *pot*), to [bo], "pretty" (*beau,* pl. *beaux*), to [mo], "word" (*mot,* pl. *mots*), to [to], "early" (*tôt*), and so on.

Most combinations of consonants and vowels in French have such characteristics and in all cases offer the possibility of ambiguity. So, the number of tools is unlimited. Furthermore, the ambiguity can appear not only in words but also in sentences. In French sentences, words are not delimited by pronunciation, there are no word boundaries, and sentences are just a succession of syllables. For example, the word *samedi*, pronounced [sam(ə)di], has the meaning "Saturday", but [sam(ə)di] can also be written as the sentence *ça me dit*, which means: "It agrees with me."

To conclude: we can have one pronunciation for more than one signification at the *letter* level, with the *syllable*, the *word* and even on the *sentence* level, which offers a wide range of possibilities for ambiguities, spoonerisms and other wordplays.

The Players

PLAYING WITH LANGUAGE is an indication of language mastery but also a technique to make a conversation livelier. To play also means to play with somebody, with somebody you know, or with somebody you don't know. In fact, communication is not so much about giving information as, first of all, about establishing contact with somebody else. In verbal communication we also articulate our emotions; so, melody, rhythm, meaning, *i.e.*, the signification of words, follow the emotional attitude of the speaker. By playing with language, the speaker may aim to amuse, to shock or seduce the hearer(s). It doesn't necessarily mean being humoristic, but it is an activity related to the spirit, an intellectual pleasure that is articulated by a smile at the end of the play. Subsequently, the success of the play depends on the hearer(s).

What is required for successful interaction is a partially homogenous competence and knowledge (linguistic and cultural) of the interlocutors, because the hearer still has to make a cognitive effort to comprehend the wordplay, he has to move from the first signification to an implicitly intended signification level. "I like Ike", for instance, is only amusing to people who are aware of the reference to President Eisenhower, otherwise it doesn't work.

As in any game, the player can lose. This problem arises if there is a lack of mutual understanding between speaker and hearer(s), which may occur for example if irony is used. Irony often involves saying the opposite of what we want to say, not with the intention of lying but to amuse through the contrast between the two opposite senses: "It is horrible!" then has the sense that something is beautiful, wonderful. But it also means that if the hearer doesn't feel the irony, he just comprehends the first sense, which is, in this case, the opposite of the intention of the speaker. So, irony can be a dangerous game, especially when (combined with amplification, exaggeration and euphemisms) it becomes confused with humor, as is mostly the case in French culture. Bearing this in mind, and also bearing in mind the fact that this is a favorite style in French communication (in particular when establishing contact with someone), misunderstandings will often occur in communication with foreign partners.

The Rules

HOW TO PLAY with language is a cultural characteristic which differs from culture to culture and from speaker to speaker, and it is limited to people who know the rules of the game. Because playing with language means using it not as the language rules demand, but deforming it and breaking with conventions.

In addition to the homonymous phenomena of the language, ambiguity can also be intentionally forced, *e.g.*, by a speaker who leaves out part of a sentence. This implicit style is typical of French communication. Two preconditions have to be met for this type of communication: firstly, the suitability of the language, in this case at the level of the syntax, and, secondly, the right attitude of the speaker. In contrast, for example, to the German language, where the verb is often at the end of the sentence, so that the listener has to wait till the end of the sentence to understand the message, in French syntax the verb goes after the subject, so that it is possible to interrupt the sentence just after the verb and produce ambiguity caused by the omission of the rest of the sentence.

This is also possible because of the "polychronic" attitude of the speakers. What does this mean? French speakers literally talk "together": when several people talk, there will be more than one conversation going on and more than one topic being discussed at the same time. So with hearers not necessarily waiting until it is their turn to respond, speakers seldom have an opportunity to finish their sentences. Due to this communication style, people develop an ability to interpret what has not yet been uttered, which means that such communication is not without ambiguity!

So these are the basic conditions of verbal communication in French culture: the language is suitable for playing with because of its implicit meanings, homophonies and ambiguities, and its polychronic speakers with their non-linear communication. All these conditions form the basis for a typical attitude and contribute to a passion for playing with language which causes French speakers, unlike people from other cultures, to avoid a neutral and direct communication style. One reason for this attitude could be historical. Rhetoric has played a big role in French culture since the first universities were established in the Middle Ages. To *persuade*, to *emote* and to *seduce*—these three functions are still present in French communication. Each decision or act is based on a sound argument, and elocution, employing the whole range of rhetorical devices, is a central instrument in verbal communication. Not what you say but how you say it has been a central element in conversation since the culture of the royal court, the goal being to persuade through pleasure and emotion supported by a stringent line of argument. Trying to make people smile is an implicit rule of sociability in France; the intention is to make people comfortable at a personal level, especially on first contact. So misunderstandings may occur, in particular, in the interaction with people who are accustomed to making a serious impression on first encounter, with people who have a direct and neutral communication style, and with people who laugh only with those whom they know. As already pointed out, irony can get people into difficult situations when they are in contact with foreigners. Seduction is another dangerous place in which to play with language.

The Play of Seduction

SEDUCTION AMOUNTS TO different things from culture to culture. In some cultures, it may be regarded as a way to chat up another person. But seduction should not automatically be equated with flirting. There are different ways to accost somebody, but while the flirt includes the element of seduction, the French play of seduction doesn't necessarily include the sexual intention of flirting. People normally live in microcosms, where they have fixed relationships (family, friends, colleagues, *etc.*). Through the play of seduction, people take the opportunity to go beyond the boundaries of their familiar world. Instead of playing only within their microcosms, they take the risk of, say, accosting foreign people of the opposite sex. This typical play is a "democratic game", because you find it everywhere in society, regardless of generation, gender or educational level. And it works on the basis of two premises. Firstly, people agree to be seen and recognized as sexual beings—and not just as the neutral human beings that they want to be or have to be in other cultures. Secondly, it works because of an implicit, agreed convention: that there is no primary sexual intention, and no aim to develop any deeper relationship.

This contradiction between sexual recognition and non-sexual intention constitutes the basis of this special type of communication, which, for this reason, merits the description "play". Seduction and games have another point in common: the creation of a world apart, which borrows its substance from the real world, but which takes us out of it at the same time. The seducer promises another life, more dazzling, more cheerful, and more sentimental. He takes us where life will take on its own momentum; we leave, with him, the familiar paths, we are far away from the world of habit. It is seen and felt as a precious moment, when somebody gives something—implicit or explicit compliments—without expecting anything in return. All that is required is the complicity of the person accosted; it means that the people involved in the interaction play on the basis of the same rules. The moment is gratis, for the amusement of all.

I remember the occasion when I was in a French bakery and asked the saleslady for two croissants. An old man (about seventy years old) who was standing beside me waiting for his turn said: "Hmm, croissants, lovely!" This exclamation can hardly be said to be very informative—everyone in France knows that croissants are tasty. However, though it fails to provide much in terms of semantics, it *does* contain two pieces of discursive information. It is an appeal for attention; and it plays the role of an introduction to the following conversation:

> The old man:"Do we eat them at my house or yours?"
>
> Isabelle: "The place doesn't matter; the point is that I have to buy one more for my husband."
>
> The old man:"Oh, you're married!"
>
> Isabelle:"Yes, I'm sorry!"
>
> The old man:"It doesn't matter!"
>
> Isabelle (to the saleslady):"So, *three* croissants please."
>
> Isabelle (to the old man):"Shall we bring him the croissant *before* or *after* we've visited your home?"
>
> (The old man and I, the saleslady and all the people in the bakery laugh.)

It was just a brief moment, just two minutes of the day; we met for the first and last time without any commitment on either side. We were the protagonists of a little play, as though in a theatre, far away from reality. The result was a win-win situation: for the public, because of the amusement, and for the old man and myself because both of us felt flattered. He felt young enough to seduce a woman, and I felt attractive enough to be seduced.

But what happened really? The amusement was caused neither on the explicit nor on the implicit level, but by the interplay between both and a third level called the intentional level, where all literal significations become obsolete. The knowledge of this third level and the complicity of all interactants made this play possible.

The point is that in other cultures the interpretation of this situation could have been different. Interpreted on the basis of the first level, I myself would have been disturbed by the forwardness of the old man, the saleswoman would have sold me three croissants, and the customers in the bakery would have regarded the old man as a disagreable person. But this type of communication doesn't carry the same negative connotations in French culture as it might in other cultures. Therefore, French speakers often have communication problems with people who are not used to seeing the intentional level of communication, as well as with people who, though they might see the different level, are not accustomed to communicating with strangers on such a personal level, because not everybody considers humor as a good way to start up a conversation.

Explicit	Argumentation	Implicit	Intention
"Lovely!"		You are lovely	(Compliment) Do you want to play?
"Your place or mine?"	Thesis => Inviting an assertion	I want to have a romantic tryst with you	Please play with me!
"It doesn't matter where!"	Assertion	I don't object	I want to play with you!
"There is a husband"	Counter-argument	There is a problem	The ball is now in your court
"You're married?"	Is this argument true?	You seem so young	(Compliment)
"It doesn't matter!"	Refutation of the argument	There is no problem	I pass the ball back to you
"Three croissants please"	Resolution and confirmation of the thesis	I say yes	Thanks for the play
"Before or after?"	Rhetorical question as conclusion	The problem is not solved	End of the play

"QUEER" OTHERNESS
BY T. W. GERAGHTY

IN THE SPRIGHTLY days of my youth, I was much taken with a certain young lady. It was a bumpy ride. She did; but then she didn't. She would; she wouldn't; she *might*. And so we had a heart-to-heart talk, and she gave me her final word on the matter—which was "no". Apparently, it wouldn't work. I pushed hard for an explanation. Both my emotions and my hormones were giving me no peace, so I needed to know. I wanted closure (naturally I was also hoping to win her over with my persuasiveness). What she then told me was that we weren't suited to each other because we were so *different*. She wanted (or needed) someone who was more like herself, someone who would understand her and give her support in the struggles of daily life, not someone who would constantly puzzle and confuse her.

I couldn't deny that we were indeed different, though, looking back, probably not as different as we thought we were. After all, we were both of us young—and green, spoilt, and self-obsessed (as young people tend to be). But she seemed to see this *difference* between us as a threat rather than an attraction. I argued as well as I could, pitting myself against a hypothetical imaginary male friend of hers whom she chose to favor over me. The two of them (being so similar) would surely bore each other to tears, I said! Whereas she and I would complement each other. I even told her the lovely fable of Aristophanes in Plato's *Symposium*, in which the comic dramatist, invited to discourse on the subject of love, recounts how Zeus once split all humans in two, since when we have been searching frantically for our "other half", our complement.

This idea of an enabling *coming together* (and I intend no erotic pun) of halves that need and complete each other is a very powerful one. Love has this in common with language (and literature), where meaning is normally created by a cooperative interactive process. In both, there is a movement of the interactants towards each other. Both love and language are carried on wings—Eros is a winged god; thoughts are "winged", famous quotations in German are *geflügelte Worte* ("winged words"), Pegasus is the winged horse of the poets, and so on. And, as the poet and classicist Ann Carson (1986) has explained:

> As [...] writer and reader bring together two halves of one meaning, so lover and beloved are matched together like two sides of one knucklebone. An intimate collusion occurs. The meaning composed is private and true and makes permanent, perfect sense (108).

Well, in theory at least.

> In fact, neither reader nor writer nor lover achieves such consummation. The words we read and the words we write never say exactly what we mean. The people we love are never just as we desire them. The two *symbola* [knucklebones broken in two to serve as tallies—*Ed.*] never perfectly match. Eros is in between (109).

Aristophanes' tale of the lovers searching for their lost other halves may be beautiful, but it is untrue! Perhaps the young lady and I would have complemented each other; more likely not. But you can't blame a man for trying.

Be that as it may, this was a formative experience in my sentimental education, and the idea of seeking *fulfilment in difference* rather than *security in sameness* remained an important maxim for me.

Now imagine my interest when, many years later, I was reading up on the (gay) British novelist E. M. Forster (1879-1970) and came upon the following, in the excellent biography of that writer by Nicola Beauman (1993):

> Middle-class gays often search out working-class lovers for the reason that someone who takes a lover of the same sex then has to *create* otherness, the other: class, and an unordered relationship, are the obvious means. This is not mere *nostalgie de la boue* [a longing for the low and degraded—*Ed.*], it is the search for difference (302, "create" emphasized in the original).

Forster, sensitive, highly educated, and with a wealthy upper-middle-class lifestyle, had a preference for intimate relationships way outside his own class, whether with the Egyptian tram-conductor Mohammed el Adl, the chauffeur "Tom", the ship's steward Frank, the stoker Charlie, or the policemen Harry Daley and (his last great love) Bob Buckingham (for more on these, see Beauman and the voluminous standard biography of Forster by P. N. Furbank).

Admittedly, many factors come together here. In the British context, the working classes were associated with virility and (rather unrealistically) assumed to be more at ease with their bodies—think Connie Chatterley and Mellors the gamekeeper in D. H. Lawrence's *Lady Chatterley's Lover* (1928), a novel strongly influenced by Forster's long-suppressed gay novel *Maurice*, which Lawrence had apparently read in manuscript (Summers 1983, 18). The non-respectable working-class men, outside the constricting bonds of middle-class values, enabled sexual license.

> In moving from their own milieu to a lower class, the homosexual writers not only transgressed against social norms but were also able to break free of inhibitions.

> Interclass relations became almost imperative to homosexual affairs [at this time]. J. A. Symonds and Oscar Wilde consorted with men from lower ranks; [Frederick "Baron Corvo"] Rolfe and Lord Alfred Douglas were partial to telegraph boys; Edward Fitzgerald established friendship with Joseph Fletcher, a Lowestoft fisherman, his "Posh"; Henry Scott Tuke painted portraits of Falmouth fisher-lads; [Walt] Whitman's relationship with Peter Doyle and Edward Carpenter's with George Merrill are well-known examples of friendship in this mold (Bakshi 1996, 65).

Then there was the factor of power and control, since the middle-class partner, with greater wealth, eloquence and social self-confidence, could more easily set the terms for the relationship. Concomitantly, though, it was hard for him to be sure that his working-class lover wasn't in it just for the material advantages; in the extreme case he might effectively be paying the man for sex.

The sexuality of another famous writer, Oscar Wilde, is a case in point. While engaging in more idealized intimate realtions with such young men of his aesthetic circle as Robert Ross and Lord Alfred Douglas, Wilde also sought the sexual company of young working-class men who were, to all intents and purposes, male prostitutes. They took his money, but then ratted on him when he was brought to trial. However, as he later wrote to Douglas in *De Profundis*:

> It was like feasting with panthers, the danger was half the excitement. I used to feel as a snake-charmer must feel when he lures the cobra to stir from the painted cloth or reed basket that holds it and makes it spread its hood (72).

Although it destroyed him, it was a thrill of Otherness that Wilde the creative artist, whose own life was perhaps his most dazzling creation, desperately needed.

Almost equally scandalous was the fall of the great French poet Paul Verlaine, whose life was altered forever in 1871, when into it burst the peculiar figure of Arthur Rimbaud. The precocious teenager was foul-mouthed and unwashed but, where "others saw nothing but a dirty, sullen lower-class boy growing out of his clothes", Verlaine "divined the charm and intelligence beyond the dirt and surly monosyllables" (Hanson / Hanson 1958, 153). Rimbaud was indeed uncontrolled and dangerous, but he was not a working-class "panther"—he was the outstanding literary genius of his generation. Verlaine abandoned his family, to embark on a bohemian peregrination—and homosexual affair—with the dirty but angelic-looking boy wonder. The adventure ended in recriminations, a shooting incident, and the humiliation, disgrace and imprisonment of Verlaine. (France being less prurient than Britain, Verlaine was gradually allowed to slip back into French society after his release from prison.)

Rimbaud had not ruined him, however. Far from it, he had *made* him:

> Rimbaud had saved Verlaine from living as so many of his Parnassian friends lived, playing at poetry from the shelter of a safe job or an adoring parent; he had forced him to balance artistic integrity against all that he loved so well—comfortable home, friends, respectability and licence neatly mixed, good feeling everywhere—and to come down on the side of the first; and he more than any other man had made Verlaine the poet (209).

Neither bourgeois security nor safe pseudo-bohemianism in the cafés of Paris could have done this. Verlaine needed that disturbing encounter with the Other, in the unhygienic form of

Rimbaud, to make him aware not only of what he was *not*, but also of what he had it in himself to *become*. Here is the truest meaning of "complement": it is not merely the supplying of what is still needed for completion, but the discovering of where within yourself that missing something can be found.

This is a phenomenon wider than the need for one French poet to be shown the way by another, for an Irish playwright to find in rough sex the liberating excitement that would inspire his creativity, or for a British novelist to experience Otherness in intimacy with someone from beyond his social class. At the height of his love for his Egyptian tram-conductor Mohammed el Adl, and seemingly in a mild state of shock, Forster confessed that the racism and narrow-mindedness to which he had previously, albeit reluctantly, fully subscribed had now broken down. In a letter to his British confidante Florence Barger dated July 18th, 1917, he wrote, "It seems to me that to be trusted, and to be trusted across the barriers of income, race and class, is the greatest reward a man can receive" (*Selected Letters*, I, 263).

The Other is queer (in the non-gay sense of the word), is radically different from yourself, and will quite likely rock your life. You will learn from the Other—indeed, the *only* way to learn is by looking into the mirror of difference—but what you'll actually discover are things about yourself. This is the only way that you can grow and, like it or not, it can only be done through encounter with the Other.

References

Bakshi, Parminder Kaur. *Distant Desire: Homoerotic Codes and the Subversion of the English Novel in E. M. Forster's Fiction*. New York: Peter Lang, 1996.

Beauman, Nicola. *Morgan: A Biography of E. M. Forster*. London: Hodder & Stoughton, 1993.

Carson, Ann. *Eros the Bittersweet* (1986). Champaign, IL: Dalkey Archive Press, 1998.

Forster, E. M. *Selected Letters*. Ed. P. N. Furbank / Mary

Lago. Volume I. London: Collins, 1983.

Furbank, P. N. *E. M. Forster: A Life* (1977-78). New York: Harcourt Brace Jovanovich, 1978.

Hanson, Lawrence / Hanson, Elisabeth. *Verlaine: Prince of Poets*. London: Chatto & Windus, 1958.

Lawrence, D. H. *Lady Chatterley's Lover* (1928). Harmondsworth, Middx.: Penguin, 1960.

Plato. "Symposium (The Banquet)." In: *Great Dialogues of Plato*. Transl. W. H. D. Rouse. New York: New American Library, 1956, 69-117.

Summers, Claude J. *E. M. Forster*. New York: Frederick Ungar, 1983.

Wilde, Oscar. *De Profundis* (written while Wilde was in prison, 1895-97). Mineola, NY: Dover, 1996.

ABOUT THE AUTHORS

Rainer Barczaitis is a retired lecturer in linguistics and translation studies at Hildesheim University, where he taught for 28 years. A trained *Germanist* and *Anglist*, Dr. Barczaitis has published on (among other topics) the translations from English into German by Arno Schmidt, who continues to be one of his favorite authors. He is an inveterate Anglophile, and a great fan of Tom Lehrer.

Ellin Burnham, a Bostonian, studied geography at Barnard College of Columbia University and international development at Harvard. Since 1995, she has been teaching English at the University of Göttingen (Germany). In her free time she works on her sort-of-*Bildungsroman* about her twenty-year-old car, "who" is also an experienced transatlantic traveller.

Jürgen Einhoff was a teacher trainer for teachers of English before retiring in 2000 and has been teaching comparative cultural studies, focusing on the USA, at the University of Hildesheim for a couple of years. He is an ardent advocate of systems theory and has published a number of articles and readers on language-teaching matters. His contribution to this volume reflects his own personal views and experiences. His London-born wife has—of course—been his greatest asset.

T. W. Geraghty is a veteran Irish writer, scholar, intercultural commentator, journalist and raconteur.

Peter Graf was professor of intercultural education at the University of Osnabrück (Germany). He is a co-founder of the Institute of Migration Research and Intercultural Studies (IMIS) and set up Osnabrück's postgraduate program in Islamic religious education. Dr. Graf retired in 2008, and now enjoys the increased opportunity for travel, for meetings with friends from other cultures, and for personal intercultural learning.

Silvia Grimmsmann grew up as an MK (missionary kid) in Central Africa. After studying intercultural communication (among other things) at the University of Hildesheim, she spent eighteen months in Greece, worked as an intercultural consultant in the Rhineland, and now lives near Berlin, teaching languages. She is into creative writing, and has a baby daughter.

Paul Harrison is a professional translator living in Berlin. When not reading and learning languages, traveling and getting to know people, he enjoys singing, writing songs and playing the ukulele.

Francis Jarman teaches comparative cultural studies and intercultural communication at the University of Hildesheim. According to family tradition, he is descended from the Thracian slave Androcles (of "Androcles and the Lion" fame). In 2009, Dr. Jarman was awarded the Erasmus Prize of the German Academic Exchange Service. He is also a playwright, novelist and classical numismatist.

Isabelle Kross teaches French language and culture at the University of Hildesheim. Born and raised in France, she married a German and has lived for some thirty years in the north of Germany, experiencing the cool efficiency of German culture, yet still suffering from the effects of seduction withdrawal.

Anne-Kristin Langner is a doctoral student in the Institute of Media and Theater, University of Hildesheim, researching into television phenomena in an intercultural context. In 2006, she was awarded a Certificate of Achievement for outstanding academic performance by the University of Nicosia, Cyprus. She also works as a journalist, writes short stories, and takes a strong interest in Swedish language and culture.

Mayuri Odedra-Straub has had the privilege of living and working in many different countries (Kenya, Zimbabwe, England, Singapore, India, Japan, Germany) and cultures. Dr. Odedra-Straub's work experience is also a rich mixture of teaching, research, consulting, publishing and raising two teenage children. Her passion for travel, and wanting to make a difference to other people's lives, made her start her company, ETOSE, which organizes ethical tours, mainly of India.

Manju Ramanan or "Mango Romanian" according to spell check has no connections with Romania. An Indian journalist with ten years' experience and an MPhil in post-colonial Canadian writing, she is currently working with Sterling Publications in Dubai Media City. She does like mangoes, however.

Guadalupe Ruiz Yepes teaches translation and interpreting at the University of Hildesheim. She has also taught translation and languages in higher education in the USA and Spain, and spent a year at Aston University (UK) doing post-doc research. Dr. Ruiz Yepes' research interests include the comparison of sauna facilities in Lower Saxony.

Hans Schmidt is an Oceanist. After trying his luck for several years as a medical translator, linguistics teacher, archivist, furniture salesman, cleaner, secretary and house husband, Dr. Schmidt now teaches translation studies at the University of Hildesheim. In his spare time he plays football and writes dictionaries of lesser-known languages.

Emilia Slavova teaches intercultural communication and other communication-related subjects at the University of Sofia (Bulgaria). She graduated in English and American studies at that university, and has also studied at Oxford (as a Visiting Chevening Scholar). Dr. Slavova's main academic interests are in politeness, intercultural communication, social history and critical discourse analysis. She lives with her family in Bulgaria, but her heart is in England.

www.ingramcontent.com/pod-product-compliance
Lightning Source LLC
Chambersburg PA
CBHW032108090426
42743CB00007B/280